THE TOP DIMENSION

VIEWING THE UPPER DIMENSIONS

PHYLLIS SINCLAIR

authorHOUSE®

AuthorHouse™
1663 Liberty Drive
Bloomington, IN 47403
www.authorhouse.com
Phone: 1 (800) 839-8640

Published by AuthorHouse   02/05/2016

ISBN: 978-1-5049-5635-2 (sc)
ISBN: 978-1-5049-5673-4 (e)

Print information available on the last page.

CHAPTER ONE

Have you ever wondered about infinite space? The universe God's playground of endless space, what's out there? It's mind boggling to say the least. Do we just come to an end? Maybe the universe is round like all the planets, there's nothing outside the sphere, but what is nothing? Isn't space itself just an open field of nothing, apart from a few stars, and other planets where are we in the realm of things? Oh! We know where we are in our own solar system, but basically we are lost in space. No one seems to mind the journey and the traveling around and around, but for me the questions are just as infinite as space itself. My mind is blazing with never-ending questions that could never be answered rationally. Astrologists tell you one thing, and the Bible tells you another, while the Government hides the truth altogether. Then again there is the possibility that there are views you or I have never heard before. This is where the journey leads us spaced out in outer space.

There was one question that seems to have been answered for me. That is, do aliens really exist? I seem to know from experience that there is such a thing as aliens. There is life after life all through the universe. I have had the pleasure on occasion of meeting up with a few aliens in spirit form, and to my acknowledgement they are as real as any entities here on earth's dimensional realm. The spiritual dimension is a place known to sleep walkers. Sleep walking through the different dimensions meeting up with all kinds of entities roaming the unknown is not an unusual thing. There's a playground out there in infinite space where sleep walking through the different dimensions seems to bring up questions, unanswerable questions. The questions seeming to be devoid of answers, and they are as infinite as space itself. The out-of-body experiences as I've come to know them by have left me pondering over the endless questions. Questions about space, and about God, about this thing we call life, about aliens, and their reason for coming to earth.

Sleepwalking has brought me to the realization that aliens are here. They have been here for many years, and they are here collecting DNA to restart our plant just in case we blow ourselves out of the universe. Here I've been shown that possibility, a possibility of blowing ourselves out of the universe. The universal timing would be around September first, twenty- thirty three- with our planet no longer existing in the solar System. However doomsday prophecy has been around since the beginning of time, and it is written that not even the angels in heaven will know the exact time of our demise.

This has nothing to do with my life or the fact that I seem to be living two lives at the same time. Maybe in my dimensional walks through the universal dimensions I have gotten insights into the fate of our plant. Maybe that is why I have been chosen to experience the far-out wonderful dimensions of our universe, and meeting up with an alien in spirit is no worse than meeting up with a stranger here on a crowded street. They seem to be our friends, and here on earth's dimension the possibility that they are here to help could mean they all follow God's universal laws. I'm not saying they are all good, or all bad, for heaven knows we haven't met them all. Personally I haven't met the earth bound aliens at all. Why would they be any different than Earth bound personalities? Personalities of people here on Earth, we have the good, and the bad, however God doesn't look at us as being good, or bad, just whether or not we make good, or bad decisions! We are not judged by God we are judged by ourselves!

As a young girl I talked to my best friend about alien life, and the wonders of the world, but it really hadn't prepared me for the living experience. I didn't realize at what age my two worlds finally collided. One day I was grounded with both feet on the ground, and the next I was searching universes of unimaginable dimensions. It was amazing. Life was amazing, life or life after life, and that we were actually living in one or the other. There seemed to be more questions than answers, answers that I very much needed to explore. Now with years of out-of-body travel, questions still remain. I'd like to say I'd found the answers, where did we all come from, but that would be afar stretch. If nothing existed after death, then there would be a large open field with nothing, however even nothing in my mind had to be something. Maybe it wasn't Noah, and the ark, but a space ship. Maybe we are implants from a different planet.

I don't know if it was from trying so hard to understand, concentrating so hard on the scientific aspects of life, as opposed to religion, that I started to sleep walk. Sleep walking was a term I preferred to call my universal journey, while it was actually journeying through different dimensions. Sleep walking apart from my body was a term known to the outside world as out-of-body experiences, or out-of-body traveling. The experience of traveling out-of-body brought about a different view of unworldly worlds, seeing apparitions not normally viewed by earthly entities. Maybe they were aliens, maybe not, but to a first time visitor, it was all alien. I can't say that I was a first time visitor, because it seemed to be a lifelong process. I don't remember any other life at all. This life style definitely had many more privileges than disadvantages. I have come to the conclusion that once before many life time's ago, the aliens may have jumped started our planet, after a large flood for example, or many eons before that. Are Adam and Eve really the mother and father of all human life? Explaining the different bloodlines is a hard one! How could so many different nationalities come from one family's bloodline?

How many do you think has ever stopped to rationalize, or analyze, the facts put forth in the Bible? For the most part it doesn't make any sense, yet it's there truth, fact, or an act of fiction. It has to be a label of truth that struck the cord with all earthlings. The cord of truth handed down too earthlings. Earthling believing in a system that started at the beginning of time, following through to what will be the end of time. Now we are subjected to believing those mighty powerful words of the creator, but are they really the words of the creator, or manmade manipulations? Ask the atheist they will tell you that it is all hogwash. Obviously it is quite plain to see that the upper dimensions are nothing like what we have been told. Strangely enough the upper dimensions are all loving, and non-judgmental, and a paradise for time travelers.

Astral –travel or out of body-travels brings us to the realization that we are living in a fictitious reality, what we believe to be real, is strangely an illusion. There is learning beyond all human speculations once you have learned to let go of the fearless-fear of the unknown, and let your spiritual body fly free above to the wondrous spiritual land—the home land, the land from which we came. Everybody can do it, practice is what it takes, practice, practice.

It's time now to do some analyzing, soul searching so to speak, time to take knowledge to a higher level, to the God Head. It's out there the all-knowing power of the universe waiting to be tapped into. It's been written that God was and always will be never changing, yet the Old Testament depicts God as a vengeful God something to reckon with, while the New Testament depicts him as a loving, forgiving, peaceful entity that all can trust and love. The God everyone is looking, searching, and longing for, isn't that what God is really all about, the learning experience? The power of learning to love, when you've mastered that, you'll find the true power of the universe, the true God, the true creator, and all the false fables will disappear.

Through the out-of-body traveling a world of knowledge unfolds, and the fables of life and life on this planet don't seem to add up. The pieces of the puzzle don't fit, and my inquisitive mind hungers for more, as my imagination runs rapid leaving me with different thoughts, and different ideas, strangely different ideas, and thoughts than any of the so called sane people of plant earth. Just to rationalize the idea that infinite space can expand with a large bang leaves my thought process wondering how something infinite can expand at all. Sure I know they are only talking about our universe expanding into infinite space, and into different universes, but still can't they just be exploring more of our universe through modern technology, and that technology might be expanding while our universe stands still. I realize that this is not feasible as everything evolves, including all universes in outer space, so expanding into infinite space is just another way of evolving, but my mind cannot phantom the works of the creator.

These were just a few of the things that came to mind as I watched my husband undressing, and redressing for bed. Soon I knew he would be asleep. He never seemed to have time to worry about the trivial little things that bogged me down. Unimportant is what he tells me my thoughts represented. I worry too much about the little things that I had no chance in Hell finding answers for. This was his response, and the response I would always get if I tried to explain my views of life, life before life, death, and life after death, and of course the big one, out-of-body travel. This however, was my life, a curse some might say, but to me it was a gift from God.

Out-of-body travel was something my husband Jack could never understand, he didn't believe it could be done. Out-of-body travel was something that fulfilled my life completely, giving me the freedom to leave my body, and explore what most only dream about. Awake I'm normal, asleep I'm gone. The traveling seemingly was making my life a two way mirror. Who says you can't live more than one life? Who says you only have one life to live? Maybe in this body having two sides to a coin, makes it seem like two lives in one, yet I'm going to flip this coin, showing you true, we only have one life, but being eternal we reside in many bodies throughout the ages, and life never dies. This may seem a little outlandish, and off the wall to those not willing to believe in reincarnation, however believe it or not, reincarnation is real. The reincarnation experience from astral travel proved more important, and beneficial than anything I've ever learned from textbooks.

I didn't feel I should change the laws of this dimension, or build a Church. (I am not another Joseph Smith.) I just wanted to write it all down, and let the chips fall where they may. This is my life's story, a story so unbelievable that even I at times feel, and see the insanity of it all. Who in their right mind could ever believe that the weird, and unusual things that happened in the past, and the things that keep happening in the present could possibly be for real? Real or unreal, a day in my life without incident was a reward in itself. Now telling it to the world opens up portals best left closed for the fear that they are signs of insanity, and insanity has its place only in an intuition, I am prepared to take that risk. This all started long before I was old enough to realize the abnormality of the situation, before I was old enough to realize, and was told that this was an impossible possibility, when I believed everybody had the power to astral project. But falling back on infancy is a road to far to travel so from this day forward, I will try to unravel the raveled.

My husband, and my children have learned to accept me, but they prefer to call me psychic, or clairvoyant never an astral traveler. To make such claim would be to admit insanity. After viewing the obituary column today, and seeing yet another relative listed with just a few words like loving, caring, and the final good-bye we'll all miss you, I knew I had to leave behind something more of myself, I had to feel that everything I'd been, and was going to be made a difference. My life had to make more of a difference than a loving, caring mom of three, a biography, or just a day-by-day account of the rest of my life. It was a yearning, a longing, a promise to myself, anything at all to leave the world in a better state of reality, whatever that reality might be.

As I lay here in bed watching storm clouds gathering in the north through the open drapes, I realize how powerful my gifts from God truly were. I was feeling the urge to fly away, leave my body, and just travel through the universe. The power had been off all day due to the impending storm. Dark heavy clouds filled the sky, and the wind had wiped things up to frenzy, leaving us without power all day. It was bed time before any sign of repairs were in the works, repairs that wasn't about to last through the night. I was restless, but astral travel only happened when I allowed my body to sleep.

I remember resetting the alarm, and even winding the wind up clock so as to make sure our day started off in the usual manner, but that just wasn't to be, so why I would expect my day to be a normal day only heaven knows. I wasn't expecting the power to flip on and off all through the night, and I wasn't expecting the wind up clock to stop somewhere between four thirty, and five o'clock. I was just trying to get to sleep, but getting to sleep was unsuccessful for now the storm had intensified. The full butt of the storm was bearing down on us, and there was a feeling our safety was in jeopardy. If the wind intensified much more our county home might wind up back in the city, and I didn't need a windstorm to carry me over the rainbow. According to my husband Jack, I had been somewhere out there all my life.

Thunder and lightning raged all night, first the horrific flashes of lightning, then the horrible roar of thunder. It was like a Steven King movie. Flashes of lightning filling the whole sky, flashes of lighting that lit up the bedroom where Jack and I were trying to sleep. Jack laughing at me for saying that the shadows that appeared on the wall seemed eerie and spooky, for they filled the whole room. We laughed, and talked, first about the shadows, then about the remote country hide away, the safe and comfortable hideaway that we had chosen to live in. It was our country home, a home full of mountains where the wild life runs free. There was a soothing mountain stream that flowed straight through our back yard making the most unbelievable, beautiful landscape that only Mother Nature herself could have possibly made. The sound of the running water that cascaded over the tiny water fall brought a restful, pleasing, and peaceful feeling. The most peaceful country living that anyone dared to imagine was right at our back door. It was a cradling song of nature that helped rock us to sleep.

If you had ever been on a camping trip where the tall pines seemed to touch the evening sky, watch the twinkling stars overhead, feel the cool evening breeze on your face, then you could imagine the comfort of our peaceful hide-away. Life was a camping trip three hundred and sixty five days a year. This was what we had always dreamed about, this was our dream home, yet in no way could our dream home compare to the beautiful scenery that unfolded once you entered the upward dimensions. Here no earthly words could describe the beauty of the unfamiliar loving territory. The colors alone were enough to take your breath away. Thousands of colors, never before seen in our dimension surmounted the endless valleys. Colors, many colors dotting the heavens where one dimension seemed to end, and the next one thundered onwards. Dimensions only a peaceful loving God could have made. Creating this scenery could only be, God, the creator, the universal power, that filled my belief system to the brim.

Now with the thunder booming above our heads, and the lighting flashing over and over around our country home, the stage was set for the ghostly activity that was about to start it's shadowy play out. A strong feeling of fear had gripped the room leaving us shaken, and afraid. Shadowy figures often roamed the halls on a night like this, shadowy dark figures that left a lot to be desired. I could see the dead that's true, but I preferred not to on such a spooky ghostly night. Jack nervously laughing, he was laughing at me, and telling me, that the only thing spooky was my wild and imaginative imagination, which seemed to peek on stormy nights, but I could see that the shadowy figures had taken over his wild imagination as well.

Jack could see dark shadows flashing in the hallway, and shadows on the bedroom wall, but he couldn't visualize them as anything other than a shadow of a tree branch, or a shadow the bedroom furniture might have made whenever the lighting flashed, and lit up the room, and I had accused him of having no imagination at all. They are plainly shadows in human form, I told him "Look" I said, as I pointed out the features that were so plain, and obvious to me, yet still he only laughed at me "Darby honey, every house we've lived in according to you is haunted." He was saying that, I thought, only to ease his own worried mind. He knew for sure that every house we had lived in had been haunted. Ghosts were like my household pets, they followed me everywhere.

Yet he was trying to convince me that this house couldn't possibly be haunted, because it was so far away from city life, or civilization as he preferred to call it. "No respectable ghost would think of living so far away from the good haunting grounds." "Face it Darby he said, we are just not important enough to have our own personal ghosts." As he was saying this he was pulling the covers up over his head, being a man he didn't want to admit that he was seeing humanly shadowy figures, big brave Jack now trembling, and shaking under the protection of the big down filled comforter. Jack my hero, my protector, my Jack, now hiding under the big blue fluffy down filled comforter. Love you Jack, I whispered as I settled back on the pile of fluffed up pillows. Three big fluffy pillows that I had placed neatly against the head board hoping to be able to read awhile.

Knowing that Jack would soon be asleep and reading would soon put me to sleep. I was sure to fall fast asleep, deep into slumber, shadows, or no shadows. However reading in the dark wasn't feasible, and my mind wondered away, far away, with memory after memory taking over, filling my restless brain as, I watched all the dancing shadows. I was watching the shadows, shadows of the dead that would soon fade, or blend into night time dreams, or nightmares, whichever the case might be, I'd soon be traveling the universal land of the unknown.

It had been ten full years now since Jack and I had moved from the city to the country. All three of our children were now grown, and living apart from us. They hadn't wanted to move from the comfort of life in the city, and now that they were grown, and gone Jack and I were free to make our own choices. These choices we made were choices of living happily ever after in the counter, just me, Jack and the spirit world. Living in the country was what we wanted more than anything. However it wasn't like settling for the first place we could find, we had put a lot of time into searching, and looking for the perfect home. The perfect home would have to be a place for growing old, and living happily ever after, and the search had taken a great amount of time. This place was ideal, and well worth the time spent in the search. Each parcel of ground here covered ten full acres, beautiful, beautiful acres. We were awe stricken with the beauty of it the very first time we saw it, and we knew this had to be our house! Fresh snow had just fallen, and covered everything in sight. The sight was that of a winter wonderland. Jack had been quite skilled as a hockey player in high school. A talent that had followed him through his college years, so here Jacks dream of building an ice skating rink became his new dream.

Jack with the patience of a saint, had taught our three children to ski, and to ice skate. He loved to take them out on the little frozen ponds and watch as they attempted to stay up-right, and made their way around the ice without falling, soon all were experts at both skiing, and ice skating. There was an attempt for me to learn also, however my skates didn't want to cooperate. There was diffidently a need for a pillow attached to my backside, here on the mountain top it would appear that ice-skating would be reincorporated into our lives.

We just had to have this property, and this wonderful house, and with all the beautiful spots this house could have been built on, it wound up on the south side property line. We realized this was the ideal place for no other spot would have captured the beautiful landscape nature had provided. Mountains and trees as far as you could see, yet it was only a few miles to where the city lights would fill the night time sky.

Here on the mountain it was the setting sun that seemed to kiss the tree tops as it made its final descent from view, leaving only the moon to shine down on the mountainous mountains. Mountainous mountains over stocked with nature's wild life, the wild life that seemed always to come to life in the night time shadows.

We were completely happy with country living. There were no close neighbors a feature however that was not long to be enjoyed, for soon after we moved in, the ten acres on the south side of us was purchased, and the biggest house ever built on this mountain side went up practically overnight. Of course they built on the same property line adjacent to our south side property line, why waste the view. The view of the beautiful mountain stream, the waterfall, and the perfect picturesque mountains filled to the brim with pine trees, a view completely alluring to all who had ever had the privilege of setting their sights on.

Soon a very large family moved into that big house, and now our space seemed a little crowded. The crowd brought with it a lot of yelling, screaming, and laughter from little children. People coming and going as the family settled in. There were bulldozers, and landscapers buzzing around bringing with it a noise that seemed to last for an eternity. The dead people were quieter than those people. Of course the dead were only known by me, and they were being very silence at the moment.

My house was haunted. Oh! Of course it was, I knew that but, the ghosts that dwelt here seemed friendly enough, and if I didn't bother them, and they didn't bother me, then for sure all living arrangements could be tolerated. On the other hand, I often wondered if our new neighbor's house was haunted also. Maybe we were all living on sacred ground, maybe our house was built on an Indian burial ground, and therefore the new neighbors would be plagued with the same unearthly spirits that occupy our home. Maybe that's who these black shadows were, restless spirits of a departed Indian tribe of long ago.

It only took me a short amount of time to realize that our house might have a few left over spirits, spirits who still wanted to enjoy our beautiful home. I often saw the shadow people in the hallway, but tonight they seemed to be having a ball. It had to be the storm there was no other explanation. Well maybe there could be a few other explanations, I'm sensitive they want my attention, they need my attention, and doing their little dance was one way, one sure way of getting my attention. Maybe that could have something to do with it. As far back as I could remember I had been able to see, and to communicate with the dead. The shadow people however seemed to be from a realm beyond my knowing, for I could only catch a glimpse of their ghostly bodies, and the shadowy figures were scary even to me. Jack often told me it was my imagination that there was no such thing as shadow people, or ghosts, and only someone with my weird imagination could make something from nothing. My imagination couldn't, and wouldn't scare him at all but, ghosts were real to me, and they were definitely coming out of the wood work tonight, so it had to be Jacks imagination that had him cowering, and shaking under the comfort of the comforter.

The cracking of thunder, the flashing of lightning, over and over again, the sound was enough to wake the dead, and it was apparent that that was exactly what it had done.

I was restless, tossing, and turning, having a tug-of-war with Jack over the covers, trying to hide my head under the covers to keep from seeing the bouncing shadows that danced their way up and down the hall, all the while Jack was telling me to stop. "Stop tossing, and turning, he would say, or go sleep on the couch." He didn't want me to pull the covers off his head. I don't know how long this went on, or when I did finally fall asleep. Sleep doesn't come easy with the rain pounding the roof like a stampede of wild horses, or when your haunted house turns into a freak show. I finally managed, however to fall into a very deep, and comfortable depth of sleep, and found myself in a dimension unlike any dimension I had ever experienced before, or so I thought, maybe I had been here before. The dream however was far beyond describing. Oh! This was such a wonderful dream. Sleep walking once again that's what I was doing. Oh—but thinking it was a dream, and knowing it was realistic make it ever so exciting.

The out-of-body dreams start the same each, and every time, someone holding my hand as I'm lead out onto a pond of ice, my feet supported by a sparkling pair of ice skates, and here, I am skating like a pro. Only in an out-of-body dream state was this possible, if I'd been awake I would now be looking at the sky from a prone position. All these fancy moves now were mine to command, even though I didn't have names for what I was doing. Dressed in the most beautiful red skating skirt, I'd skate until the guide holding my hand, and I came to the new horizon there, I'd enter the next dimension fully dressed in a flowing gown of white bathed in a brilliant white light. These changes come without notice. Suddenly it's me looking like a beautiful movie star. How on earth—no I can't say earth, this is too spectacular to be earth.

Having a wonderful dream even though you are frightened out of your wits seems a little unreal, yet there it was, unfolding into a magnificent experience, an experience that when put into earthly words, and terms, could never be explained. We weren't alone here, there were people everywhere, and the sounds of beautiful music filled the air. This was something that everyone needed to hear, for no earthly sound had ever captured such clarity, and beauty. No voice on earth had ever sung the words of this beautiful song. The scenery itself seemed to be humming a peaceful welcoming tune. I felt that I had actually died, and gone to heaven, but I knew I hadn't really died. It was just another walk in the clouds. Here in this dimension there are no ghosts, only spirits, loving spirits, helpful spirits. Spirits giving me the capacity to love, and be loved, and though I wanted to call them spirit they preferred to be called the living life force, or the source. So what are we as earthly entities, but living life forces, or the source waiting to happen!

I hadn't realized how lonely life could get when suddenly you're left without the sounds of children running through the house. Lonely when you're up rooted from the hustle and bustle of city life, even though it was a well thought out plan to do so. The sounds of the children next door, their laughter, and their playful voices, were a sudden reminder. Sometimes it was just a lonely, lonely, feeling missing my children. Being lonely didn't have to be an option in my life though, for the spirit world was always close at hand. Beautiful cloud bursts of spiritual blessings. Beautiful, spiritual blessings, was what I liked to call it.

There was a spirit visitation from one or more on a weekly basis, and never had I been afraid. Some had become regulars for whatever reasons of their own, reasons I wasn't sure of because I hadn't thought to ask. My only hopes here were that they wouldn't give up for I really enjoyed their visits. These were the things I needed to reveal about my life, but how could I do such a thing, and still sound sane. I would talk to Jack about these things, but he didn't seem to listen, so I hadn't felt that he really believed me. It was my world of make believe, he would tell me, my childhood fantasies, the world of dreams that should have been long forgotten. My guess here was he hoped I would forget, but that just wasn't happening. This world was as real to me as the mountains, and trees outside our bedroom window. It was a life within a life, and I was living in two dimensions at once. It was like living two life times at once, to fulfill one earthly obligation.

When you spend most of your time alone with only the land of the dead, sometimes you start to fit right in, and you start to wonder what your obligations really are. You sometimes believe that you too are among the dead, and the life of the living is the unnatural state of being, especially when you find out you are the living life source waiting to happen. How is it possible to help either dimension? The dreamland is just another ghostly reality, but dreaming is what makes life bearable for the lonely, anyway that's what did it for me. My dreams were my reality, and tonight my dreams had me flying, flying from one dimension to another, talking to people who had long ago left the earthly realm. My parents, my brother, sister, and other departed relatives that I hadn't seen in many years, all now a part of the living life source. Being in spirit was the only way that I would ever be able to contact these people, because once they had crossed over, my ability to make contact with these people was gone. The Earth-Bound Ghosts were my specialty.

All I wanted to do was stay here forever. It was like reviewing my childhood remembering the love that had filled our home when I was a toddler. There was someone new with me now! I was dreaming, I had recognized that, but who was this person controlling this dream journey I was taking, this universal walk in a bubble of light, and love, leading me onwards? Wow! It was another spirit guide, my spirit guide, and this spirit guide was guiding me deeper through this dream dimension. I saw the earth below as I seemed to fly higher and higher, my new guide by my side, he was showing me the different dimensions, and they were so beautiful. I was imaging this only as a dream and, waking up from such a place would be a big disappointment. If I could I would dream here forever. I was beginning to realize it as a reoccurring dream, one that I had had many times before, yet not until I was fully in the middle of it did I remember, and waking up was not a thing that I would cherish. I was thinking it must have been the high frequency from the lightning that picked me up, and deposited me in this wonderful dreaming dreamland. My guide by my side shaking his head, and telling me it's not a dream, you're really here, and it was your guides who brought you here. However no speech was needed, or necessary here, they always knew what you were thinking.

This was a night never to be forgotten, for all through the night we walked on beaches that sparkled like gold beneath our feet. We watched the stars that shown in the heavens, stars that were like little birds we could catch, and hold in our hands, giving us light to fly by in the night sky. My spirit guide showing me how everything in the universe was alive. In the upper dimensions there is no death anywhere, just living, loving entities, of spiritual light. Even the flowers gave off a beautiful humming sound that vibrated of peace, giving the impression that they were happy just to be, always alive, always a flower. We traveled through dimension after dimension, we talked about the top dimension were very few were ever spiritual enough to exist. It's a Godly place where not knowing maybe even God himself exists. I don't know why I was given the opportunity to meet, and to talk, to my loved ones that had long ago left the earthly realm. Talking to my loved ones living in one of the other dimensions, was still a guessing game. I couldn't tell you where, or why, any of this was possible, it just was. I had the impression that even Jesus himself was standing in our mist, for there was a loving light that shown so bright, a love that felt so right, but never a face, just a feeling of pure love so unlike anything the earthly realm had to offer. It was unbelievable, and a scene that would be almost impossible to describe to my children. I was being told that human spirit life usually didn't inhabit these lower realms, or dimensions, which we were seeing here tonight. It was just a special reminder for my dormant memory, a dormant memory, I had been suppressing now for a very long time. Here I was being told, was a much needed reunion back to spirit from a very long vacation, a vacation I really didn't remember taking.

Sometime during the night was when the power left the premises for an amount of time unknown. The thunder and lightning was what finally woke me from my wonderland of sleep. The clock radio was flashing twelve, the sky through the partly open drapes gave the appearance that it was still the middle of night, yet I knew we had over slept, and Jack was going to be late. There were hospital rounds to make before his regular day of scheduled appointments. Jack didn't like keeping his patients waiting, and now he would be in a panic knowing that when it rained this hard, for this long, the roads would be flooded, traffic would be backed up, and there would be no way he could make the twenty miles to the hospital, and still be on time. We had been through this before.

Jack was just an intern when we met, fell in love, and started a family, but with the greatest of all ambitions. With his strong ambitions, and the mind set to become a doctor he endeavored. The struggles were long, and hard, and many times we thought maybe this wasn't the life for us, yet he prevailed. He was a good looking intern, and even better looking as a doctor. I have to admit he melted my heart, and set my life in spin cycle the very first time we met. Six foot one, dark brown hair, and twinkling blue eyes, eyes that twinkled whenever he looked at me, was I lucky or what? Here I was just an aid in the hospital pharmacy. Always thinking myself to be quite plain, at five foot four, long dish water blonde hair, and hazel eyes, shy and awkward, but hoping somehow he would notice me. Well he noticed, and we knew after the first date that we were meant to be together. We dated for three months before we decided that two could live cheaper than one, and the rest was history.

Love, romance, and the start of the family life, married, and very soon thereafter, married with children. Still now after twenty six years of marriage, we lived the life of the newlyweds, for there is never a day that he doesn't remind me of his love for me, and how much he misses me when duty calls, and he has to spend time away from home.

There is always a kiss or the gentle caress of his hand whenever he comes near me. Where on earth has there ever been a love like this. It had to be a marriage made in heaven. In heaven, where the pre-life-planning, decides your earthly plight, and decides the life path, you will take. Maybe we do choose our life path before we leave Heavens realm, but it's always a surprise to wake up, and a little disappointing when time is up, and it's time to return, leaving heaven for earth. Now being fully awake, and back from Oz, the drab existence of being human, living the earthling life again, I'd have to hurry wake up Jack, and start life again in this earthly existence.

Now here I was shaking him while he was trying to be romantic, pulling me down kissing my neck, and begging me to let him sleep just ten minutes longer. "No Jack it's late. Jack will you please wake up?" That's all I could say, I hit him with a pillow to make sure he was fully awake, and then paused long enough to drag out my dream diary. I had to keep track of my dreams no matter how late we were. I still couldn't believe that it was anything more than a dream. If my dreams weren't of an unearthly phenomenal nature then they were simply a regular dream, and a regular dream could vanish away quite quickly. I needed these notes, for memory was fast to fail me. Somehow referring back, I would find little clues, clues for future events, and sometimes clues that I had somehow over looked from the past. As I begun to write I realized last night really wasn't just a dream, it was one of those wild walking dreams from the past that I sometimes took. The walking dreams that I never talked about even to Jack for they all seemed to be nothing more than a dream. Last night's adventure proved to be more than a dream, however it was an actual walk in another dimension. How could I have ever forgotten the beauty the other dimensions had to offer, I vowed never to do that again! I'd make sure to make lots of notes so as not to forget a single detail of this adventure. It was an adventure like Peter Pan and Wendy! Sprinkle a little fairy dust, and off you go. Maybe you have done this yourself, you go to sleep, the next thing you know you have left your sleeping body far behind, and you are off on the journey of a life time.

This dream was not one that could be wasted either, each and every detail had to be recorded. It wasn't likely that I would forget this dream this time. Maybe in the past I had disregarded the experience as just a dream, maybe in the past it was just a dream. This time there was no way I would be forgetting any of it. I was making mental notes as well as written detailed notes. When you have an experience like this, you know you have to capture it all. It may be a year, or two, or maybe never before anything like this would ever happen again. My only hope was that when nighttime came around again I'd be able to continue the dream to the end. "Have you ever had a dream that actually had an ending?" That happened to me once, it took two full nights to complete the dream, but on the second night it ended much the same way a good movie would. The dream now, I don't remember, but the experience is one I will never forget.

I often speak to my diary as though it were a real person, so the entry's that I make each day is like writing to a friend, for a while the diary was my only friend. Then Lucy, and her husband Steve Spencer, moved in next door, next door being the big house, the house which was built adjacent to our south side property line.

Now just like life in the city we had neighbors, close neighbors. Soon I found neighbors very rewarding, I wasn't spending so much of my time alone, and I had Lucy. It was several months after they moved in that I finally found the nerve to ask Lucy if their house was haunted. She told me that since she had such a large family it would be difficult to notice, and she jokingly laughed off my question without asking why I had asked her such a dumb question. She hadn't thought to ask me if my house was haunted, but somehow it started all our conversations on the paranormal.

Lucy was such a good listener, listening to all I had to say. I talked, she listened. I told her everything I knew, about everything I knew. It was her facial expressions that really cracked me up. If I talked about something sad, her facial expression was that of the sad sack puppy dog. Something happy and she was smiling a large happy smile. Something really depressing, she seemed to pucker as though she wanted to cry. It was though I was giving her a script to read, and she had to audition for the part. Such a cute young thing she was, small, and petite, natural blonde hair with eyes as dark as the night. I had never seen such dark eyes on a natural blonde before. I can't say she was beautiful, but she definitely was a cutie, a personality plus. She couldn't have been over five foot tall or weighed over a hundred and five pounds. I think I was jealous, and I think the feature I was most jealous of was her bosom, very voluptuous. All the outfits she chose to wear certainly highlighted her in all the right places. Wow! Could she be any more perfect?

Lucy became my best friend always there like one of the shadow people that roamed my hallway. She was a very good friend, and someone I could talk to at any time. Lucy was someone that could talk to me, and I would listen. We spent each and every morning sitting at my kitchen table drinking coffee, and eating powdered sugar doughnuts, much to the unknowing of her Mormon husband Steve. We talked about things that I had never mentioned to anyone, and I'm sure that some of the things she told me were meant to be kept in complete confidence as well. The fact that she was drinking coffee was another issue altogether. There was never a coffee pot to be found in a Mormon household, according to her husband Steve, and it didn't matter that Lucy was Mormon only by marriage. Mormon or not, she wasn't allowed to have a coffee pot.

Steve and Lucy didn't seem like the perfect matched couple in my opinion, nothing at all like Jack and me. He was a heavy duty burly kind of a guy; huge muscles, not at all tall, but short and stout, and looked like he could have taken on Michael Tyson in face to face combat, or hand to hand whatever. Definitely not someone you would want as an enemy. Lucy was infatuated with this rough and ready lustful over sexed bully, so who was I to say? Maybe they were meant to be. They had their dreams, and I had mine, and though my dreams were mostly night time dreams they were still dreams.

This morning with the dream still fresh in my mind, I couldn't put my dream diary down. I had to capture the whole dream, it was so spectacular, and I wrote that this has probably happened to almost every living soul at least once or twice in a life time; it's just that they don't remember, that's why it's so important to keep a dream diary.

The diary was never meant for anybody to read but, me and why I wrote like I was writing to a pen pal is a little unusual I'll admit. It was my invisible friend so to speak, so I wrote like there would soon be an answer in return. Instead of calling the diary, a diary, I called it my Dream Genie, so instead of saying Dear Diary, I would start with saying Dear Genie, and then the writing would become more of a personal friend to friend communication. I'll catch you later Genie, I wrote, I have much more I need to tell you about. That was my last entry into the diary before Jack yelled at me. "Darby, coffee, get the coffee made." "Don't bother with breakfast. I'll pick up something later." He had already gathered himself up, and headed for the shower. Laying the diary down, I was thinking, this isn't something anybody could forget about. I'd have time to write more later, if anyone had ever had this experience they would remember, I'll remember, I was sure I'd remember, so the rush was on to get Jack ready, and off to work. However the nagging feeling was still there. I had disregarded these experiences as dreams before. I would just have to keep reminding myself of the reality, and not let myself forget.

CHAPTER TWO

———◆———

Just as I started to fill the coffee pot, I heard Jack screaming about no hot water. The power must have been off for quite some time. It had to have been off for hours if we didn't have any hot water. The hot water tank in this house was huge. The whole house was huge, and a lonely-lonely place for a doctor's wife when the doctor was away, which was a great deal of the time. It seemed that the hospital where Jack spent most of his days, and most of his nights, required his presents more than his home life. Maybe that's why I seemed to be living in a fantasy world, a world far apart from the hospital in a haunted remote country setting, where the haunting seemed to increase with the power of a good mid-summer storm.

We hadn't had a storm like this one for a very long time there just didn't seem to be any letup in its rage. The wind was howling, the thunder still rolling, and the lightning still cutting its way from heaven to earth. Now Jack in the shower who usually whistled while he showered was making a little singing song that sounded something like burr, burr, burr, grumbling all the while about the cold water.

"Okay! Hon," "No hot water" I was yelling at him now, "If there's no hot water then you'll just have more time to get ready for work." "Make your shower shorter!" "That's funny Darby, he said,

I'm freezing to death here." "This water is freezing, really-really freezing." "Cold showers are more invigorating Jack." "They really have a way of perking you up." "And I supposed that is funny to you too Darby!" He was grumbling but the shower was still running, and I knew he wasn't going to leave the house without showering, shaving, and brushing his teeth. It was the morning ritual, complete with a fresh lay out of clean cloths. I guess that's why I loved him so much, he had to shine like a new silver dollar each and every morning, although this morning, I was sure his shower would be a great deal shorter. Cleanliness was always the first priority of all health professionals, and health providers, but there was a scrub room at the hospital where this task was an ongoing ritual, and hot water was never a problem.

About the time the coffee began to perk, the phone started to ring. "Hello," I answered. "Hello Mom, I just called to wish you a happy birthday." It was Sandra, my beautiful daughter. "Thank you Sandy, today is my birthday isn't it, I forgot!" "How could you forget your birthday, Mom?" "Didn't Dad remind you a few hundred times?" No Sandy, I guess he forgot too." "Not likely Mom, he never forgets a birthday, a holiday, or any special occasion." "You know Dad." "He is always on top of everything." "Are you coming to see me Sandy" I always had to ask her even though I knew what she was going to say. "To far Mom can't make it, but I'll come see you real soon I promise." "Have you heard from either of my brothers?" "Not yet, but if you remembered, I'm sure they remembered." "Well I'm sure Dad remembered too, Mom, she said, you'll probably get a truck load of flowers delivered to your door any minute now." As she was talking the doorbell started to chime, not once, but several times like some impatient person couldn't wait for someone to make it to the door. "Well the door bell is ringing Sandy, so maybe your right." "I'll see if your Dad will answer it for me." "Jack will you see who's at the door?" "I've got to go anyway Mom, she said, it's time for me to get ready for work, so go get those flowers." "See you soon, I love you." "Love you to Sandy, bye." "Goodbye Mom, have a happy birthday!"

I could just see Sandy in my mind's eye probably standing there talking on the phone dripping wet from her early morning shower, wrapped in a large bath towel. Her long wet blonde hair would now be dripping in a puddle on the floor. This was a scene I had seen, so many times when she was a teenager. As I was hanging up the phone, I called out to Jack again to answer the door. "Jack will you answer the door please." He was standing in the bedroom doorway now, fiddling with his neck tie. "Hon, I don't have time." "I don't have time for any of your invisible friends I'm late." "What do you mean, invisible friends, Jack?" "I mean the people you talk too, that no one else can see." "That's not fair Jack, I don't talk too invisible people." "You do Darby." "You do it all the time." He was yelling back at me now from inside the bed room, all the while the doorbell chimes were still sounding off. "Sometimes you look like that guy for Quantum Leap, he was saying, Sam I think his name is, you know the guy that talks to the hologram." "Well I guess you'll just have to tell me when I'm doing that Jack, because they all look alike to me." "Even you honey, I called back. You look like a hologram to me." I knew he wasn't going to answer the door now, and since Sandy had already hung up, and the coffee had already started to perk, I had no more excuses. I'd have to be the one to see who was there. It was much too early for Lucy. She had to take care of her family before she could come over. That would be awhile since she had a very large family, and tending to them would take a great deal of time.

I open the door, and much to my surprise, I found Megan standing there. Megan was a young lady that I had met shortly after Jack and I had moved here ten years before. "Hello Megan what are you doing out in the rain?" As I was asking her, I noticed that she didn't appear to be extremely wet, even though she was dressed in a skimpy little yellow dress, no coat, no umbrella, a pair of sandals, giving the appearance that she was on her way to a summer picnic.

"I was just walking by, she said, and I noticed your newspaper about to float away so here." She handed the paper to me. "Do you want to come in?" She was shaking her head, and saying no at the same time. "No Tommy will be wondering where I am, I have to go." Tommy was her boyfriend, and they had been living together ever since I had known her. "I think your friend Lucy will be coming over in a few minutes." She said. "You think so?" I asked. I knew Lucy would be over. Lucy being a coffee drinker always knew the coffee was on at my house. Still I was wondering why Meagan thought that Lucy would soon come over, she had never met Lucy. I had told her many times about the wonderful friend next door, but still she always ran away before I had time to introduce them, and now she was about to do the same thing again. "Well Megan said "She's been in and out of her house several times already." "The first time she came out, she ran right back, and came out with an umbrella, then back in, and out with a big box, then several times just in and out for no reason that I could see." "She hasn't been out for a while, but I'm sure she will come out soon." Megan said all that without taking a breath, then turned, and started walking away. She was walking away without even saying goodbye. I yelled goodbye to her, and she turned to wave. I waved back, and then noticed Jack was standing by my side. He wasn't saying anything. He just kissed me on the forehead.

"Can you believe that?" I was asking Jack. "Megan out in the rain dressed like that!" I opened the door a little wider so he could get a better view. "Dressed like what?" He asked. "Megan," I was answering. "Megan, she was dressed in a little summer outfit." A puzzled look came across Jack's face as he stepped out the door for a closer look. A second later he was back in closing the door. "Darby you really do worry me sometimes." "And you're doing it now!" "There is no one out there!" "Honey there is no one out there!" "I know you've talked about Megan for a long time, but nobody but you have seen her, don't you think that's a little odd?" "No, I answered, I can see her, she is real." But Jack insisted that she was one of my invisible friends, and he teasingly said. "Well she appears to be Casper the Friendly Ghost to me!"

This could not be, not Meagan, I had known her forever. We've had many heart to heart talks. We had talked about her life, about Tommy, and about this house. It was the house her folks had lived in before Jack and I moved in. We've talked about how her family had abandoned her after she moved in with her boyfriend Tommy. It just couldn't be that she was one of the invisible people that Jack had accused me of talking too, but why then wasn't she wet, why did she look so real?

I knew that Jack was just trying to screw with my mind. If she was a ghost, or a spirit, why did she look so real? She looked as real as Jack himself. I must be losing it or my ability to see, and talk, to the dead had defiantly improved. I had never known a ghost to look so real. If she was invisible to Jack then she had to be a ghost, or spirit, or one of those holograms. "Look Jack, I said she brought me the newspaper, how could a ghost do that?" "I don't know honey." He answered. "I just know there was no one there." "You need help!"

Jack was hugging me now looking at me with troubled eyes. "I really do think you need to talk to someone about all the things you see, and hear Darby, I'm concerned about you." Jack's voice was a little worrisome, but I assured him there was nothing to fear. "I'm alright Jack." "Although, I do wonder why you haven't said anything before." "You wait twenty six years to tell me you think I fell out of the coo-coo nest." "Honey, I don't think you fell out of the coo-coo nest, but I do think you are teetering on the edge." "I think you need to see a shrink." "Darby dear, I didn't wait twenty six years to tell you this." "I have told you that before!" "Jack you think I'm crazy, I asked?" "No honey, you just worry me when you talk to thin air like there was really someone there." "There was someone there Jack, I said. Megan was there, and she is real." My brain was buzzing now puzzling over Megan, I had been talking to this girl for ten years now, and never once did she appear to be a spirit. "Jack I think it's time for you to go to work." That's all I could think of in my confusion to say to him. He was smiling at me as he grabbed a couple of powdered sugar doughnuts form the box on the table. "I'm taking half of your doughnuts honey, that means Lucy will probably only stay half the day." He filled his coffee mug then gave me a quick kiss on the cheek. "Got to go, he grinned I'll call you later." "Go Jack get out of here!"

A shudder ran through me as I got the strangest feeling, it was a feeling that Jack wasn't going to be safe. Something was wrong, and sometimes I would get strange feelings, feelings that I didn't understand, but always when something bad was about to happen. I'd feel something was wrong, but it would seem these messages came from the beyond. "Wait Jack, wait!" I was practically screaming at him. He couldn't leave not until I knew why I was getting this feeling! It had something to do with all the rain maybe the car. "I think you should take my car." "Why is that?" Jack wanted to know. "Because it's bigger, and you can get through the floods much easier, what do you think?" "Your car is so small sometimes it stalls in the floods, I don't think it's safe." "Anything else I should know miss psychic?" "Well yes there is, you need to take an umbrella!" "Darby dear, the car is in the garage, I park in a parking garage, how wet do you think I'm going to get?" "I don't know Jack, I answered, I just feel you should take one." "When I get these feelings there is always a reason." "Okay, I'll take an umbrella, but you do know that if there is a reason, the same reason will require me to use both hands, so I will need someone to hold the darn thing." "Want to come along?" The door was closing behind him as he was talking. He was gone now, and I was alone, he hadn't said happy birthday, and there wasn't any flower delivery. He didn't take the umbrella, however he did take the bigger car.

Now with a cup of coffee in front of me, and waiting for Lucy, I started thinking about what Jack had said about my mental condition, and I was thinking maybe I did need help. It couldn't hurt having a little help sorting out the real from the unreal, but I knew I was not completely out of whack. I had had these abilities all my life, being able to talk to the dead was a gift. I loved the weird and unusual things that were forever happening in my life, all except for the shadow people, I didn't care much for them. I thought that I could distinguish the flesh and bones form the spirit, but maybe I was wrong. If Megan was a spirit she definitely had me fooled. I wanted to discuss these things with Jack, but how could I. He already believed I needed professional help. He had even mentioned that I see a psychiatrist or a shrink as he called it. He had a good friend, a doctor by the name of Warren Elliott. A good friend who would give a big discount on all the sessions I might need. Jack had mentioned Warren Elliott a few times in the past, but I just refused to listen. If only I could make Jack understand, I didn't need to see a psychiatrist, all I needed was a little understanding from my loving husband. Understanding wasn't something you could get from a psychiatrist like Warren Elliott. I had never met Warren Elliott, but I knew what a psychiatrist was like. I knew that they only believe in the five senses, never willing to see beyond the five senses, which seemed to me like wasting time, and money in the office of a psychiatrist. Being psychic myself I realized life had a fuller agenda. I didn't need a psychiatrist. Whenever I needed to talk to somebody, I could always count on Lucy.

Warren Elliott's job was only to convince me that I was crazy, and that my problems all stemmed from being born into a dysfunctional family. I'm different I'll admit, I've always been different, and if Jack couldn't except me for that after twenty six years of marriage, then it was just too late, he would just have to live with it. Thinking back on it now, I knew that Jack had been living with it. For twenty six years now, he had been living with it. He was just to loving, and caring to say much, or anything about it. Maybe I should take his feeling into consideration. Maybe I should see his friend the shrink.

I was remembering when it all started, or at least when I think it all started, I was five years old. I had a little brother age three, crippled from birth, unable to move from his bed, unable to talk, or play, only at night he'd be there standing by my bed. I use to think these where just dreams he couldn't possibly be there. Yet there he was, he'd take me by the hand, and we would spend the rest of the night running, laughing, and playing, like normal children. At the age of three he died. I was devastated, and heart broken, I had lost a very special part of me, a friend, a playmate, a little brother. The preacher that gave his eulogy was saying. "Now he runs, and plays with the little animals in heaven." Being five I didn't understand any of this, I didn't understand death, I only knew I wanted my little brother back, so I prayed. "Dear God, if my little brother is running, and playing in heaven please send him back to me." Of course all knows Gods answer to that, or do they? Things are not always what they seem especially when you're a dream walker, and prayers are sometimes answered if you believe. Maybe not right away, maybe not the way you would expect, but answered just the same. All I had was my hopes someday I'd wake up and he would be there, what a foolish five year old I was. Whatever you can hold in your mind as truth, I was told, becomes truth, see it, hold onto to it, believe just believe. I don't know if this is Gods answer to prayer, or just the law of attraction fulfilling our every wish and command.

Now I knew these experiences with my little brother had to be the same as the one last night. They were out of body experiences walking in the outer dimensions. At first I just went along with where the experiences would take me, but as I learned more, and more about the dream world, I found that I could control where I wanted to go by a single thought process, of course this came at a much later time in my life, but I would think I need to see my spirit guide, and without hesitation my guide would be there. Like last night, but now I knew for certain that these experiences were real, anyone, and everyone that I could ever think of would show themselves if I thought about seeing them. I couldn't seem to find my little brother though. I had no clue as where he had gone. My Guardian Angel was one that I thought about a lot, I really liked talking to her, she told me, her name was Alice. My spirit guide would just say names are not important, but it was important to me, and I know someday he would tell me his. Why had I waited until now to realize that these experiences were for real, and not just a figment of my imagination? There was so many people I could have contacted, to many places I could have gone, so many wonderful things I could have done. It all had to have stemmed from hearing over and over again how impossible all this was. It's impossible, it's impossible, and now I need a Shrink!

Thinking back on it now it seemed like such a waste, I could have been having the time of my life, and learning about the universe at the same time, how wonderful it would have been venturing out upon the unknown frontier, meeting up with other venturing entities, whoever they may have been, Aliens' maybe. Seeing how infinite the universe really was, seeing if the infinite universe was really round like the planets, or if there was truly no end to the never-ending universe.

In time, I started to grow older, and I finally started to let go of the memories of my little brother. It wasn't a complete letting go, I still had the memories folded, and tucked neatly away somewhere deep in my subconscious. It wasn't until I was much older that I learned that letting go was what the dead appreciated from the living the most. To be let go meant they could move on into the beyond. Heaven maybe, after last night, I knew that that was the best of all places to be. Strangely now, I was coming into the realization that I had never known before, wondering why it had taken so long. Once you realize you are more than a human body, the possibilities are endless, and I knew now my life was about to change. Adrian my little brother's body was frail, and weak, but his sprit was bright, strong, and everlasting, and somewhere out there he lives.

I was on my second cup of coffee before Lucy finally showed up. She had her umbrella which she closed, and placed in the umbrella stand by the front door, and under her arm was a box, not a real big box, but a box nonetheless. Megan was right. "What do you have there Lucy?" I asked. "Ha!" She said, "I thought you would already know knowing you." "Well I don't so out with it." "It's for the birthday girl." I took the box from her and placed it on the table. She like always headed for the coffee pot. "Oh you know I'm not supposed to be drinking this coffee." "If Steve knew I was drinking coffee with you every morning he would be over here with a shot gun."

My reply to that was "Like we've said many times before Lucy, what Steve doesn't know won't hurt him." "Have I ever told you that before I married Steve I didn't belong to the Mormon Church?" She was asking me a question that she knew I already knew **the** answer too. "Awe, many, many times girl." We both laughed because talking about Steve and the Mormon Church was the one topic that we talked about most. My opinion doesn't count here, I was telling her, but I really can't see a woman belonging to an organization like that. "That's alright Darby, she would say, I feel that way too." "I especially feel that way today." "Steven wants to know why I'm not pregnant again, our babies are a year old, and he thinks I should be in the family way by now." "You didn't tell him, did you?" "Oh! Hell no, she answered, If Steve knew I was taking birth control, he would throw me out for good."

The birth control pills had been my idea. Lucy was pregnant with twins a little over a year ago when she and Steve moved in next door. With one set of twins, and six singles already running around, I thought there should be a stopper somewhere. My intentions were good, but being the Good Samaritan and meddlesome neighbor that I was, I proceeded to interfere. When I confronted her about it, I found out that she felt the same way. It was Steve she was afraid of, he thought all Mormon families should be has large as humanly possible, and as long as she was of childbearing age she should be reproducing. I could have been minding my own business, but the girl needed help. Having a mother-in-law living with her just wasn't enough.

Steve was a pharmacist and would know a birth control pill when he saw it, so Lucy had to hide her pills here at my house. I can still see a very nervous Lucy the day we went to the doctor's office to get her the prescription. She kept asking me what name she should use, also what address she should use, she didn't want Steve to find out what she was doing. "If I use my name it will show up in the computer, and he'll see it." She said, "If I use our address the bill will come, and he'll see that." "What should I do?" "I don't know, Sarah Randall is a good name how about that?" "You can use my address, now how would that be?" I just gave her the first name I thought of, but she liked it, so now Lucy was listed in the pharmacist computer as Sarah Randall, and now Sarah Randall's birth control pills were in the top drawer below my coffee pot, another reason for an early morning visit. It seemed that one pill a day was easier to hide than the whole container.

She sat her coffee cup down on the table, and grabbed a doughnut. She shoved the present toward me, and asked, "You want to open this?" "Well of course." I answered, "It's the first present I've gotten today." She kind of giggled a little as she reminded me that the day was early yet, and there was bound to be a few more. "I'm not sure about that Lucy, I said, Jack didn't remember to say happy birthday before he left today." "Oh well, to hell with Jack, open the damn present." She seemed a little agitated that I hadn't opened her package yet, so I took it, and carefully unwrapped the box. Inside the box was a Ouija board.

Just as I had finished opening the box the wind started to howl, and the branches of a large tree outside my kitchen window started scratching at the glass. Lucy jumped so fast that her coffee went splashing to the floor, and we both had to laugh at what had just happened. The thought that just opening a box with a Ouija board could bring the spirits howling in, gave her goose bumps, and frighten her. "Maybe this present wasn't such a good idea," she said at last. She was frantically wiping at the spilt coffee with a paper towel, and then when all was clean, and shining again, she refilled her cup. "I feel I'm going to need an extra pot of this stuff today," she said, "My nerves are about shot already, you know she went on, with the power being off last night, my morning routine was a complete disaster." "I was beginning to think I was never going to get things done." "I'll bet I had to retrace my steps a hundred times." Well that was what explained Megan's comment on Lucy bouncing in and out. The power being off had caused her problems as well. Well the power was on now, and we could perk coffee all-day if we needed too.

"Lucy this is a Ouija board?" I was a little puzzled to think she really believed that I would use a Ouija board. Me of all the people in the world using Ouija boards! "I have questions I need answers to, too Darby, I just thought that since you were so close to the spirits, and the world beyond, that I could get the answers a lot faster. Please don't say no to my gift!" "Well I do have a Ouija board already Lucy." I told her. "They aren't the best thing in the world to play with. You just can't trust the kind of spirit that might come through, but if you want to chance it, we'll do it."

"Lucy I asked, did you happen to see Megan on my doorstep this morning?" Lucy just gave a little nod of the head, and said. "No just you, talking to your newspaper." Wow! I thought, Jack must be right; I really am talking to invisible people! I told Lucy about the experience I had had with Megan earlier, and she took it all in believing everything I was telling her, not doubting a single word, assuring me that we could find all the answers through the board. I'm not sure why I agreed to take on the whole wide world of the dead. The dead were usually there to take me on. "We're talking about a big back yard here" I said. "Once you open the gate the yard fills up." I used to play with the board in my younger days, and found that there were more spirits waiting in line to talk, more waiting than I cared to talk too. It was spirits that wanted help in contacting the living, which to me put a brand new twist on things. Usually it's the living wanting to be connected to the dead.

I was agreeing with Lucy, but reluctantly. Before I would consider talking to the board with Lucy, I had to let Lucy know just how I really felt about it, and that wasn't good, so I told her that she had better believe in the good, and not to dwell on the negative. It's the law of the board what you believe it to be, will be. This comment was an old comment from a long ago past, but for some reason still rings true.

So many people believe that you open up a portal to the underworld, and that evil dwells within, and for many that view holds true. However my previous experience with spirit left me thinking differently. I try to view it now as opening the gates to heaven, and all the good spirit with messages for their loved ones here on earth will come to you, of course this too was from the previous experiences.

They all want your help for one reason or another, but that's something I thought we could deal with. I don't believe I have ever had a real bad experience, yet I put the board away many years ago, never to think about again, but then why shouldn't I have, the spirits knew how to find me, they knew my reputation as a medium. I didn't need a Ouija board, I was an open channel, and one that any Earth bound spirit could talk too. I couldn't blame my medium ship on the Ouija board however, because it started long before--I'm guessing from birth.

Now I had to deal with a friend, a friend of ten years that I was just learning might be in spirit. Megan in spirit must truly be after someone to talk too. She may not even know what it is. Sometimes they don't realize they are dead, and vice-versa, the medium sometimes doesn't recognize the dead. I was still not sure that Megan was a ghost. Even if Megan is dead, she certainly didn't appear dead. Not to me, but now it seemed more of a possibility than not. Ten years I had known her, and never once had she agreed to speak to anyone but me. Whenever someone else was around she seemed to disappear, something I actually never noticed until now, and now she was the topic of conversation, the topic of the day.

I wanted so desperately to change the subject that I brought out my genie book, and read the passages that I had recorded from last night's dream. Lucy was really intrigued. Spirit Guides and Guardian Angels was something she hadn't heard much about. Out of body travel was another one that baffles her, and now she was begging me to teach her how to do this on her own! All I could tell her was meditation, which was something that I may not have been good at myself. My out of body travel came automatically with the help of my guides. We have the most beautiful spot on earth for meditation, I told her, we have the beautiful nature made scenery our backyards provides, and that would be the perfect place to lose yourself in meditation.

"Lucy I said, you seem so depressed today. Why are you feeling so depressed?" Lucy was stirring her coffee nervously staring down at her doughnut, and fidgeting in her chair as though she expected Steve to pop up behind her at any minute. "Okay! Darby," she answered finally, "but you know I don't want to wreck your day, after all this is your day." "It's just that I can't take much more," she was saying. "I'm listening Lucy, tell me about it" "It's Steve, today he told me he was going to bring a second wife into our home if I didn't start reproducing real soon." "He's telling me since the twins are a year old now it's time for more." "I can't, she said, and-and, I won't." "I just can't think about having another baby." "I don't know if he is serious about a second wife, or not, but you know some of his Mormon friends believe in polygamy, and they are telling him, it is the thing to do." "I love him, and I don't want to lose him, but I can't stand to think of him with another woman." She threw her spoon down on the table, and sat there waiting for a reply. I wasn't sure what to say, but finally, I found myself telling her just what I was thinking.

"You know Lucy, I wanted to sound convincing as I told her, I think it's a bluff, he's trying to scare you into keeping your life in turmoil, I think you should call his bluff." "Say go ahead Steve, make my day." "Then don't forget to tell him if he chooses to bring in a second wife, then she should be willing to raise the ten that are already here." "Tell him you don't believe in a man having two wives, so you will simply have to leave." "You can't stick around with another wife in the house." "Say Steve if you bring another wife into my home, I'm leaving, and I'm definitely leaving alone." "I'm sure he will have a second thought, or maybe more, don't let him scare you." "He doesn't want to lose you, he loves you." "There is no second wife that wants to take on two sets of twins, and six other children so just be brave." "Bluffing is the only way!"

Lucy was talking about her mother-in-law when she said, Margie isn't going to be around forever, she helps me with the kids now, but what about ten, or fifteen years from now when I'll still have a house full of little ones, and no way to escape even for an early morning coffee break. Which was what she was doing now, she had left her mother-in-law in charge of all the littlest children. The older ones were off to school, and hopefully the smaller ones were still sleeping. "Lucy, I said, you really do sound depressed." She poured a little more cream into her coffee, now there was more cream than coffee, and she stirred and stirred. There was a little sobbing sound coming from her as she finally began to share her feelings. "Wouldn't you be depressed, Darby if you were married to someone like Steve?" "He's off bragging to everyone about how many kids he has had, and he hasn't had any of them." "He just wants to keep me pregnant, and barefoot home keeping house like a good little house wife while he goes about having a life." "I'm so tired, and I can't take it anymore." "Oh yes! His mother is getting old, and getting on my nerves too"

I had to assure her that there wouldn't be any little ones ten or fifteen years from now, because we were on the pill! So after her third cup of coffee she was feeling good enough to talk about

Megan. We kind of agreed to wait a few days to try the Ouija board. I wanted to make sure she was in a positive mood before conjuring up, or stirring up the dead, and maybe the weather would be more cooperative. I didn't want to scare Lucy again.

We did however want to talk about the dead. Lucy was always interested in the paranormal, and since that was almost an obsession with me it made for a good morning conversation. She wanted to know all the secrets of how to contact the dead, and how to tell if they were good or evil. Of course I had my own views on the dead, and the living, whether they were good or evil. I explained that I thought the dead were the same on the other side as they were when living here, so I told her. "If they were evil here they will definitely be evil there." "They carry their personality with them when they go." "It's just that God doesn't what the evil ones in his dimension, so he lets them wonder around here." She knew however that I was joking, the ones that are still in our dimension, are the ones that refuse to leave. We had talked about this before, and of course it was just my belief system, but I would tell her that when the dead had unfinished business here they would tend to stick around until they could solve it, then they would move on into the next dimension.

I knew I wasn't alone in this belief system, I had heard this from quite a few sources before, but still I wanted to believe it to be my very own. My belief system was subject to change with view after view that I had heard from other sources. For example the term Shadow people came to me from the radio talk show, Coast to Coast. It fit the little devils in my hallway so perfectly that I soon adopted the term. I knew for sure they weren't shadows of tree branches, and they weren't my over active, imaginative imagination. They were shadow people.

Lucy started asking me questions about the different dimensions, she said, she had heard so much about them, but didn't quite understand how we could be living in a parallel reality, with dimension after dimension right here in our space and time.

"You keep talking about these dimensions, Darby. What are they exactly?" I guessed that was a fair question, so I was hoping that I could clarify it for her. Anyway I was going to make an attempt. "It's like this, I said, I've heard from the time I was a small child, that we have eleven dimensions here on earth." "After contacting my spirit guide last night, and referring back to my dream diary, I now know that there are more, many more." "A dimension is just another reality, we are in one, the spirits are in another, and each one is a little better place than the last." "The higher dimension you reach the more magnificent it becomes, but there are dimensions that even the angels are not allowed into." "How do you know that?" She asked. "Personally I don't, I told her." I've only my spirit guide to rely on for information, but that's what makes it so wonderful, those out of body walks into another dimension." "That's what I was doing last night as I slept, I was in the same dimension as my mother and father, I haven't seen them for a long time, so being there talking to them was a miracle, a miracle worth holding onto forever." "The upper dimensions are as real as the one we live in, it's just that they vibrate on a higher frequency than the one we live in." "If we could raise our vibration to that level, we could walk right in." "We could see, and hear it all." "It was a gift that long ago the world possessed but has long forgotten about." "I'm sure I was telling her, as the earth gets closer to end times, these things will reappear."

How long we talked about the other dimensions was unknown. I was just so wrapped up in my dreams that I must have tried over and over again to describe the beauty of it all. All the conversations that I had written down in my dream book that once I thought was just a dream, was now reality. These conversations really did take place. I was just more or less in denial, I knew it now, and these were the conversations that I was referring to. If only I had known how real the other dimensions were, and how real the Spirit Guides, and Guardian Angels, really where, I could have profited more from my dimensional dreams. So Lucy with meditation maybe you will master these dimensions better than I ever could. Just practice, practice and never give up.

It wasn't long before our conversation turned back to Megan. Megan was so real to me that it would take a lot of convincing to make me believe she was a ghost. I still couldn't believe a ghost could pick up a newspaper. I couldn't believe that anybody as real looking as Megan could possibly be a ghost. I was really starting to feel the confusion of my mental ability. There was just too much going on in my brain to grasp it all. I was thinking of Jack, and I was thinking of Warren Elliott. Whatever was I going to do?

It was Lucy that brought me back down to earth. It was Lucy that was staying in focus with the conversation, and still talking about Megan. "If you don't want to ask the Ouija board about Meagan maybe we could go to the library," she said. "There should be information there telling us if anyone has ever died here on this property." "Well that's a good idea Lucy, but since Megan moved in with her boyfriend Tommy, it may not have been this property." "It could be anywhere on this mountain side, or just anywhere." "Then how about last names do you have any?" She didn't stop with that question, she was on a roll. "You said you moved here ten years ago, start there research back until you find something." "Don't you think that would work?" "Tell you what Lucy, tomorrow we will do the Ouija board if we don't get any answers then we can research the library." "You know I'm really excited about that Ouija board, Darby." Lucy said, then she continued saying, with your ability I'm sure we can get anything we want to know." "Not so, I told her, if you want to know the future you'll have to visit a psychic that has the ability to see beyond where my abilities end." "I have a real good friend that has these abilities, when she gives you a reading she goes into a trance, and the spirits that talk to her, tells her, your future. She's great, she charges a very small fee, but you come away knowing what to expect. You'll have a much better understanding of life, and about life after death." I can't do that, the spirits that talk to me only wants what they want, and they don't care about what I want." "I'll take you to see her someday if you'd like to go." "What's her name, Lucy asked, where does she live, she asked, when we can go see her?" Lucy was starting to bubble over with excitement. I hadn't seen her so excited ever.

"Charlotte Hutchinson." "I was remembering Charlotte, I hadn't thought of her in a long time, and now since her name had been mentioned there was a sense of urgency, I felt the need to see her too. "She lives about a hundred miles from here, but we could drive there in a little over an hour." "What town does she live in?" The questions just kept coming. "A little town called Whispering Willow." "Is that in Oregon?" "No that's in Idaho." "I want to go, I want to go." I had to laugh, "Okay, okay, I said, I'll call her and make an appointment, you can either go there, or she can come here, she'll give you a good reading I'm sure." That was the last we talked about Charlotte, because now the phone was ringing. The caller ID said the call was coming from Gnome Valley Memorial Hospital, so my first thought was, either Jack hadn't gotten to work yet, or he forgot his cell phone. "Hello." "Oh hello Jack, what's going on?" I talked to him for a while then hung up. "What's on the Doctors mind?" Lucy asked. "Did he remember your birthday?" "He just wanted me to know that I was right about the umbrella I wanted him to take this morning," I told her. "He saw a car wreck on his way to work, and he had to get out in the rain to help get a lady out of her car." "But what he really wanted me to know was that he was right too." "It would have taken three hands to keep him from getting wet." "Sometimes he just likes to irritate me about being psychic." "Well what about the umbrella, Lucy asked, did it keep him from getting wet?" "No, I laughed, he didn't take one, so he deserved to get wet."

Lucy and I talked for a little while longer, first about one thing, then another, and finally it was time for her to go home. Now it was just me and my big house. I cleaned the kitchen, made the bed, and settled down to do the alone thing. Read a while, got out my paints, and painted a while, watched television a while. The radio was a good late night companion which I liked to listen to. The all night talk show on Coast to Coast, of course was what I listened to most, but only when Jack was away. He didn't believe in any of the weird, and unusual topic's the talk show hosts on Coast to Coast talked about. Now me, I loved a good ghost story, and the entire weird, and unusual topic's, on Coast to Coast, so Coast to Coast was like having another friend to talk too. Tonight it seemed, was going to be one of those nights when I could listen all night if I wanted too. Jack had called once more to inform me that he was going to be late.

The clock showed five thirty p.m. I put the book down that I was reading, looked out the window to see if the weather had cleared, and noticed more than a few cars pulling into our drive way. First I saw my oldest son, then the other son, then my daughter who told me she couldn't be here today because it was so far, and Jack all arriving at the same time. They had planned a surprise birthday party, no wonder I hadn't heard from anybody. Cake, ice-cream, presents, balloons, the works, it was a big surprise. Even Steve and Lucy from next door showed up. Lucy had known about this all day, and hadn't uttered a word. They all stayed for a couple of hours partying, and laughing, and having a good time, and then it was time for all to leave. Sandy wanted to stay since she lived so far away. My two sons Ken and Don took their family and left, but not until they had taken dozens of pictures with their flash cameras. Jack had a special gift for me, but he had waited for all to leave. His special gift was an appointment to see his friend, Warren Elliot. I was mortified, what a way to ruin a perfect day. What was he thinking? It was a gift that he thought I'd be most pleased with, but then why did I feel so betrayed. Was it because he thought I was a nut? Maybe by appointment time I'd feel much better, but right then I didn't want to talk about it. I didn't want Sandy to know about this gift. What would she think--Mom needs a shrink?

The next day after Sandra had left for home, and life again was silent. Lucy and I took out the Ouija board. We didn't have anyone to write down the messages, so we decided to record what was coming through. It only took about a minute before the planchette started to move. We had agreed to say a little prayer, and asked that only the good spiritual entities be allowed to enter. We were amazed at the speed, and at the messages that we were getting. Lucy had agreed to leave her troubles behind, and ask only about Megan. The first thing that came through gave the message, "Megan's Mom" then stopped, then again it started to move, message two was simply just one word "fire." The messages didn't make much sense, and didn't leave us much closer to knowing the truth than before. We kept working however, and got one finally message confirming that there was a fire, and it was at Tommy's house. Lucy looked horrified. "Do you think Megan could have died in a fire at Tommy's house?" "That's certainly what it sounds like." I answered. "It will surly give us something to work on, let's try again." "Tommy, where is Tommy, we asked?" For the longest time the plancette didn't move, so we found ourselves asking the same question over, and over again, finally an answer. "Gone, gone with Megan." "Oh my," Lucy gasped. "You think that means Tommy is dead too!" That would be my guess!" I answered, being a little disheartened at the thought, but he still had to be hanging around, because Lucy had said he was waiting for her. Both of them must still believe they are alive.

We weren't quite ready to give up our quest to find answers, so the questioning began again. "Where is Megan's Mom?" "Still here" was the answer. "Still here where, where is she, where is Megan's Mom, and still the answer came back, right here." Lucy eyes were dilated with fear as she looked at me with a strained expression. "Your house really is haunted, so what are you going to do?" "You've never been alone in this house, and I think we should get a priest over here to get rid of your ghosts." Lucy was talking non-stop, and I had to shake her to settle her down. "No Lucy, it just means that now I know who the black shadows are that roam the halls." "You have ghosts in your halls, how can you live like that? "I've told you that I've always attracted spirits." "I can't move and get away from them, they are everywhere I go." "This time I've moved in on them, this was their home." "Speaking of their, do you mean you think that her dad is still here too." "They didn't abandon Megan." "They just died?" "Could be, I'm not sure!" Was all I had to say.

It was several days later before Lucy, and I finally went to the library to look for answers. We asked if anybody had ever heard of a fire on Pine Hill Road, and the answer was. "No." Our next question then was could we please look through old issues of the Gnome Valley Gazette. Maybe we could find answers there. That's when our search through clip after clip of micro film began. We knew it had to be before the last ten years, so the search started there, and ran backwards. Not finding anything we went back day after day, two weeks straight we went back before we finally found what we were looking for. I flipping the machine through page after page of newspaper clippings until Lucy yelled, "I found it." I ran over to the machine she was working on, and there it was. The date was June 24, 1976. Headlines, Large Fire on Pine Hill Road Claims the Lives of Six. Reading down we discovered the six were Tommy's mother, father, brother, sister, Tommy and Megan. The article read blaze claims the lives of all occupants. There were no saviors in a blaze of a newly constructed home located on Pine Hill Road. The blaze could be seen high above the mountain tops emanating above Pine Hill Road, a blaze that threaten forest land, and wild life habitat, and claiming the lives of all six occupants of the newly constructed home. No cause for the blaze has yet been determined.

The date now was April 17, 2004 that meant I'd been talking to someone who had been dead for twenty-eight years. I'd been sharing a home ten years now with Megan's dead mother, maybe her father as well, we still needed to find out what happened to them. We didn't want to start scanning obituaries. The journey through the piles of newspapers had been long enough.

However we decided we needed to help Megan and Tommy, and whoever else might still inhabit that property. We had to help them move on to the loving light that they should have gone to twenty-eight years before. This was not going to be easy. First we had to convince them they were dead. Then there was the problem of Mr. and Mrs. Thornton. Thornton being the name offered as a casualty for one Megan Thornton, in the article dated June 24, 1976. Tommy's family name had been listed as Warrick. We now had something to go forward with. Hopefully we could find some way to help.

Charlotte Huchinson specialty was sending spirits into the light, so my guess was she would be the best person, I could contact for help. I told Lucy that I would phone Charlotte, and see if she had the time to come help with our little problem. "Little problem, little problem" Lucy was screaming at me. "It may be a little problem to you, but to me it's a big problem." "I'm not real fond of having ghosts running around, they scare me to death." "Why!--Can't you get into the spirit of things?" I asked. "Hopefully not." she answered. "I have too many things left to do before its spirit time."

At least she still had a sense of humor. She had been dying too contact the dead, and now that she had succeeded, she tells me she is scared to death, well she would just have to get over it, because we had gone the distance, and there was no turning back now. It would have been helpful however to know how long it had been since the Thornton's had died, and if they truly were hanging around, or did they just come back because we summons them from the dead. Were they the black shadows that I had seen in the hallway the night of the big storm? These were questions that had to be left to Charlotte. However Charlotte couldn't come right away, it would be two weeks before she could clear her schedule long enough to make the trip. Lucy and I however started our search once again at the library. We found that both Mr. and Mrs. Thornton had died of natural causes. Mr. Thornton's obituary claimed he had died May 28, 1989. Mrs. Thornton on January 20, 1992. They hadn't abandoned their daughter, they had just simply passed away, or they just simply passed. It seems they didn't go away.

CHAPTER THREE

Lucy and I where both waiting anxiously for the day Charlotte would finally arrived. We had to have gone through two pots of coffee, and a full box of powdered sugar doughnuts in our anticipation. Of course we didn't give her any details about the house. We wanted to see what if anything she had to say. There was plenty for her to say, and she seemed to be on the same track as Lucy, and I had been. She walked through the entire house before she said a word. Then she told us that there were two people that frequented the property quite often. They knew of my ability to talk to the dead, and that they were trying to get me to give a message to their daughter. "They're not here all the time, I asked?" "No they're telling me they know when their daughter will be coming around, and that is the times they are here also."

"They tell me that they love the wonderful place they live in now, and they would never leave there except they know that Megan needs their help." "Is Megan their daughter?" Charlotte wanted to know. "Yes she is," I answered. "Well I'm not getting her, I've tried, but she isn't coming through." "She doesn't come around very often," I told Charlotte. "So tell me what message they want me to give her." "Basically I think they want you to convey the fact that she is no longer of this realm, and that she should go into the light." "If she were here, I could help you with that." "Her parents are waiting for her on the other side."

Lucy and I both thanked Charlotte. We were more than pleased to learn there wasn't anything sinister going on. Finding out from Charlotte that there wasn't any evil spirits hanging around, and that there was nothing to worry about, even on spooky nights was a big relief. That seemed to be a big relief for Lucy too. "It's still scary though, Lucy said. "Knowing that some force is watching you, doesn't that just give you the creeps?" Charlotte and I both laughed at the same time, but didn't answer her question. Lucy had more questions she was dying to ask. "Why don't her parents tell her themselves they are all dead, can't they tell her to go to the light?" "Can't the dead talk to the dead?" Even though my view of the answers was much the same as Charlotte's, I believe she answered them quite well. For here is what she told her. "Megan thinks she is still alive therefore she can't hear, or talk to the dead, and she can talk to the living only if the living believes they can talk to the dead." "That's why she can talk to Darby." "Well how about Tommy he's dead?" "That's true, Charlotte answered, but he still believes he's alive, so they are both in the same reality zone."

"Why do Megan's parents come here as dark shadows?" That's what I wanted to know. "They are the bright light of the heavenly Angels, Charlotte said, they wear the cloak of shadow to hide their brightness, they feel that will not scare you as much as their extremely bright astral body." "They are truly straight from Heaven, and their light or any light does not cast a shadow, so they cover themselves with the cloak of shadow." "Light does not cast a shadow. Are you sure, I asked?" "I can only relay what they say, and that is what they are saying." "Light does not cast a shadow." "Wow, that's amazing!"

"The belief system is a funny thing, and reality is nothing more than a belief pattern." Charlotte was explaining this to Lucy. "If you want reality to change, change your belief pattern." "You've probably heard that whatever you hold in your mind, as truth, becomes truth" she was saying. "Well believe me it works." After the long day of ghost hunting, Charlotte was going to spend the night with me, so she offered Lucy a free spiritual reading.

My kitchen table was set up for three people complete with chips, dips, and white candles, we were prepared for the reading that Charlotte was about to give. We, however weren't prepared for the messages we were about to receive. Charlotte asked us what message we would like to receive. Lucy of course wanted to know all about the threats that Steve was making. Charlotte bowed her head, and was silent for a few seconds then her voice took on a different tone as she began channeling the Akashic Records. Now she speaks, "Steve's pre-birth charts indicates that he did indeed wish to have a very large family, however he knew before coming into earthly form that ten would be the magic number, at first this saddened him, but he agreed." "Later in his new life he is living now, he would see, and be pleased with the decision to stop at ten." "The charts were showing him that putting his children through high school, and college would be a great burden." "He sees this clearly in his pre-birth charts." "I have to say even though he has forgotten about his pre-birth charts; he still desires the large family."

Now Lucy had more questions. "What is the Akashic Records, and how do you find them when going into spirit?" Charlotte's reply was simple and to the point. "They are found in the Akashic Library." Then she went on to explain how the library works. "It's not like a normal library, the records are kept on scrolls much like that of the Jester that rolls out scrolls of parchment paper in front of a King." "The difference, the scrolls located in the Akashic Library seem to be alive, you don't have to read what's printed when you roll them out, you see, and feel the whole story." "Every spirit body has a scroll each to their own, all their past, and future lives are in this library." "Anything you want to know about this life, or past life, maybe even a future life will be there. Of course that is, if there is going to be a future life, then it will be found there." "The future is on an iffy scale!"

So we plan our lives before we come to earth Lucy wanted to know. "That appears to be the plan." "I can only convey what I am being shown." "Well then why is it that some souls get stuck in this dimension?" Charlotte paused for a second more, and then she answered. "All souls are met and given the chance to enter the light, but some are afraid, and they refuse to go to the light, however none will remain in this dimension forever." "Angels either in heaven, or on earth, will soon help those souls cross over."

Lucy was so happy to find out that Steve had been bluffing when he told her he would bring in a second wife, also that since he was a good law abiding citizen he would do nothing to jeopardize his good reputation. The whole evening went quite well for we got all the answers we needed, and they were the answers we wanted to hear. We even found out that the Ouija Board was safe as long as we prayed for the white light of protection before we started asking questions, which was exactly what we had done. Now we had a green light, and the word go. Lucy didn't have to have any more kids. Her life could become her own, if she believed it could be. However, Charlotte did advise us to use a lot of caution when playing with the Ouija Board, she reminded us that it was usually the lower entities that pushed their way in to answer questions, and most people didn't know how to use proper protection. She said the best thing to rely on, was our own abilities, and if that didn't work, we could call her back. A lit white candle was advised too. White candles she told us gives off energy that good spirits could pick up on easier.

She also told us that she relied mostly on her clients own mental thoughts, when giving a reading. She is convinced that all individual entities, carry the blue print for their life in their subconscious mind, and she is just tapping into their thoughts. The advice she gives her clients is all in their mind, and is all she needs in giving readings. Channeling wasn't something that she normally did, even though it was one of her God given talents.

The next morning I thanked Charlotte over and over again, making sure she knew how much we appreciated all the help she had given us. She left before Lucy had a chance to come over, but she asked me to tell her how glad she was that she was able to help. Lucy was sad that she had missed her, for she too felt she had found a new friend. "Charlotte told me to tell you not to worry about anything Lucy." "She said she would come back real soon." "She's such a wonderful person, Lucy said, I hope she does come back real soon." "I've never known two people in this world like the two of you." "Well I guess that makes us even then Lucy, I answered, because I have never known anyone in this world who would listen to all my tales of ghosts, and nonsense like you."

"Just think Lucy, talking to you is free." "I have an appointment in two weeks with Warren Elliott, and he is going to charge me a hundred dollars an hour to listen to my tales." Lucy laughed, "And that's a discount." "That's what he said, that's a discount." That's a super big discount." "Jack said that was a big discount, and well worth the price." "Why don't you send Jack then?" She was kind of giggling her little giggle again as she spoke with her mouth full of doughnut. She went on to say, "I think he needs therapy more than you do." I thanked her, and told her I thought she was a good friend for saying such a thing.

Lucy and I agreed that we should take Charlotte's advice, and put away the Ouija board. The Ouija board took too much time, and energy to find the answers we were looking for. We still had our morning chats over a pot of coffee, and a box of powdered sugar doughnuts. I would talk about my dimensional flights, and Lucy would talk about her ten kids.

Lucy and I felt that we had made a great connection with Megan's mother, and father, and that they were satisfied with knowing we were going to help in any way we could. Charlotte made us feel that we were the earth bound Angels that were needed to help Megan cross over.

I was hoping that the Thornton's realized that we planned to help, and they could rest in peace, or whatever it is spirits do on the other side. Charlotte had told us that they seemed satisfied with the connection that they had made with us, and she had assured them that we would do whatever it takes to convince Megan to move on.

Megan wasn't about to move on without Tommy, we knew that, and Tommy didn't ever leave the property that claimed the lives of his family, he was always so busy looking for his mother and father, that the task wasn't going to be an easy one. Somehow we would have to convince both Tommy and Megan at the same time. Convince both of them that their parents had moved on, and that both their parents were waiting for them.

The property that was once the home of the Warrick's now had a new house, and a new family living there, so why was it that Tommy and Megan were still thinking they were living in the home of the Warrick's? Were they seeing a different reality? Was the new family seeing, and hearing ghostly activity? These questions and more were questions that Lucy and I were dying to find out about. But all questions about Megan and Tommy had to put on hold for now the time had come for me to go for my first appointment with Warren Elliott. Thinking about that appointment was putting me under a lot of strain, I couldn't think about much else. I visualized myself traveling out of body to the city. I wanted to get a glimpse first hand of what was about to happen. Somehow I found myself standing by my side, I had done it, and I was wide awake. The only problem with that was it scared me so that the traveling didn't take place, and I soon became one with my body once again. Wow! What a rush, and at that moment I knew I'd have to try that again. This out of body traveling was for real, and now I knew you didn't have to be a sleep, or dead, to soar with the eagles. What a strange universe we live in, it seems the sky isn't limited to the possibilities and potentials. All the wonders of the world are out there waiting for our arrival. Why I wondered had these things been suppressed!

I was realizing that my dilemma was stress related, and that the stressful thing here was worrying about the outcome of a visit to a physiatrist. Would he be thinking because I claim to be a medium, I needed to be committed! My reality check here was just to forget about it, and let the outcome speak for itself, if that was at all possible.

CHAPTER FOUR

As I was getting ready to go for my first appointment with Warren Elliott I was starting to feel a little anxiety attack coming on. My palms were sweaty, and my knees were weak. I felt like I was going to pass out at any moment. How was I ever going to get through such a humiliation? At this point in time I was despising Jack. How could he have ever done such a thing to me! I would go, I would show him, I'm not a coward.

The drive to town only made the anxiety a little worse. By the time I finally found Warren's office I was a nervous wreck. I was reading the information on his door and felt I should turn around and run, but it was too late to run, for now the door opened, and a young man came out. He looked a mess, his hair was tussled, and he looked like he hadn't shaved in days, or slept in weeks. He said hello to me, and walked on down the hall to the elevator, soon he was gone. I was wondering now should I, or shouldn't I, the thought of running was still foremost in my mind. The receptionist from inside was motioning me in. "Hello, come in," she said. She informed me that the young man had been Mr. Elliott's last patient, and now it was my turn. Once inside my first impression was, is this really a psychiatrist's office. Wow! It didn't look anything like I had expected it to look. There was no leather couch to lie down on, only a couple of real plush recliners. Mr. Elliott himself was seated in a very comfortable nice looking leather chair. "Doctor

Elliott," he said, as he stood for a few seconds to introduce himself then returned to his chair.

"Darby, Darby Mathews," was my reply. "I'm Jack's wife" "Yes, yes I know, please have a chair." I found a comfortable recliner to sit down on, and I sat there looking at the Doctor not saying a word. I was thinking this wasn't going to be so bad. This man was absolutely gorgeous. He was tall, dark, and handsome, with the prettiest blue eyes. I loved those beautiful blue eyes. This must be my weakness I was thinking. The tall, the dark, the good looking, wasn't that the exact same thing I'd seen in Jack! I don't know how long I sat silently just taking him in. He wasn't saying anything, nor was I. He was tapping a pencil on a large note pad. Finally he broke the silence. "You can sit there he said, or you can talk to me, it's your choice, it'll all cost the same." "What am I supposed to say Doctor?" I asked, "I don't know what you what from me." "Aren't you supposed to ask me questions?" "Yes I suppose I am, but first I need to know a little about you, and what is troubling you." "If you don't want to talk then we both have a problem."

"By the way doctor is too formal, he said, you can call me Warren." I'll call you Darby if that's alright with you." "That's fine with me Doctor, a, a Warren I mean." "I never did care much about being called Mrs. Jack Mathews, or Mrs. Mathews for that matter. It seems a woman loses her identity when she marries." "No one seems to remember she has a name of her own." I don't know why I volunteered all that useless information it just seemed to come out. I had only to blame it on my nervousness which must have been obvious to the doctor because he was telling me to relax. "Relax, Darby he said, take a deep breath, and talk to me like I was your best friend." I kind of laughed to myself when he said that, because I was remembering telling Lucy I could talk to her without paying the one hundred dollar an hour fee, but he did seem quite friendly, and I did have an immediate liking for this perfectly good looking stranger.

I must have sat there again for a while without talking because he was breaking the silence once more. "Darby, talk to me." "What do you want me to talk about?" "Anything, everything, could be something of whatever you feel like talking about." "Why are you here?" "I'm here because Jack thinks I'm crazy." "No, no, no! We don't use that word here." He was shaking his pencil at me as he spoke. "So let's start over." "Start with Jack if you want, but remember it's not Jack we're talking about, its Darby." "Now what does Darby think?"

"I see ghosts, and people think that that's not a normal thing, I talk to the dead this doesn't seem to be a normal thing either." "Jack tells me that I was supposed to give up the invisible friends when I was a child, carrying them into adulthood is not a normal thing." "Well, Warren said, we are not here to find out what Jack thinks, or what other people think, so from now on we are going to talk about what it is that troubles you." "If we have to analyze Jack then the price goes up."

"Warren, I asked, do you believe in life after death?" "I believe in life Darby, he answered, I'm not too sure about life after death, that hasn't been proven to me." "Why do you ask such a question?" "Darby, are you afraid of dying?" "Oh no, I answered it's just that that is a big part of my life, the one thing I talk about most, the thing that sets me off as being different, and the reason I guess I'm here." "Well then he said, I think we have a start." He was scribbling on his note pad not stopping to look up. I was beginning to think I shouldn't have mentioned it at all, and I was sure he was writing Darby is afraid of dying. "Tell me more," he glanced up long enough for me to see his blue piercing eyes, and I felt that he could already see deep down into my soul." "You believe in life after death, he was saying, we need to find out why, and also what thought process went wrong that started you thinking along those lines." "We need to analyze all your thoughts, and then we'll be able to fix what went wrong."

"First of all I don't feel that anything in my life has gone wrong, Doctor." "It's Jack, he's the one that thinks I need your help." I was feeling a little agitated as I spoke. I see ghosts, I talk to the dead, I visit faraway places via out-of-body experiences, this isn't normal in anyway, but it happens. I don't understand how it happens it just does." "These are the things that bothers all the so called normal people in my life, but to me it is just away of life, I live it every day it's no big deal." "Well, if there is such a thing as a ghost he said, then it's my guess that there is life after death." "I personally haven't ever met a ghost." "I have never traveled out of body." "I haven't done anything other than the normal day by day living." He paused long enough to make some notes on his paper then looked up at me once more, and smiled. "That means Darby that you are going to have to enlighten me on the abnormalities of the spirit world." "The information you are giving me is very new to me, but interesting." "Life in itself is strange so anything stranger could still possibly be a reality, we won't rule it out." "Now if you will tell me everything you know about the spirit world maybe we can come to a mutual understanding."

"I would like to know how to travel out of body, tell me Darby, how do you do that?" "I don't know, I answered. I've only been able to travel out of body in my dream state." "I've tried to travel while awake but, nothing seems to happen." "I'm working on that one." "A lot has happened in my dreams Warren, I said, and without my dream diary by my bedside I would have forgotten most of it." "My Spirit Guides whom I love, I could have forgotten about, and my Guardian Angel Alice, I could have forgotten about her too." "It all starts right after I fall asleep." "I see myself sitting in a swing, and it starts to swing back and forth, higher and higher, until I'm swinging through the clouds, then I'm met by my guide, that's when we skate off on slivery colored ice skates where the sky is the limit, yet there is no limit." "When you think you've come to the end, you enter into another dimension. Things change, but there is always another horizon. There are many more horizons off in the distance, with more of the unknown to explore."

I found that it was really easy to talk to this man he seemed to be interested in what I had to say, and I was telling him everything. I told him about Megan, about the fire, about Charlotte, and Lucy, about the lives that were destroyed in the fire and how I thought my house was haunted. When I had finished telling all that, he simply said "That's a lot to take in!" I was realizing he hadn't believed one single word of what I had just told him, for now he seemed to be demanding more proof. "Tell me why you think all this is a reality." "Make a believer out of me." This was his response, and I was thinking how could I possible do that? How could I make a believer out of a skeptic? I knew he just wanted me to pour out my heart and soul, so he could analyze me. Once I had started talking to him, and he seemed to be such an easy listener, and there didn't seem to be anyway to stop me. The anxiety that I had felt early had somehow subsided. I started to ramble, why couldn't I just stop? All the weird thoughts that had ever crossed my mind were coming out, thoughts that didn't pertain to anything, thoughts that would in no way help my spiritual view on life, or my life in general.

"Haven't you noticed that more and more people are talking about these things?" I was asking him. "These things aren't so far off the wall anymore." "I think we are getting closer and closer to the prophecy of what the Bible calls end times, and people are getting more spiritual, they are seeing things they've never seen before." "The veils between the different dimensions are so thin now that we are able to see, and hear, things never before imagined." "I've had these abilities for as long as I can remember, but now more and more people are having the same sensations." "I haven't talked about them to anybody except my friend Lucy, and you can see why!" "It's my belief that other people who have had these experiences haven't talked about them either, for the same reason, the fear of winding up in a place like this, or worse in a mental institution."

"Why do you feel we are getting close to end times?" I had to look at Warren for a while before I could answer him. How could he think we were not? "Doesn't it seem obvious?" These weren't the issues I had planned to discuss, but here we were so why not go for it. "Please don't think that this is one of my everyday thought processes because it isn't, it isn't something I dwell on ever, it seems that according to the Bible every time we take God out of the picture, it isn't long before he follows suit, and takes us out." "You do know Darby, he replied, every generation as far back as the beginning of time has believed that we are in end times!" "Yes, yes, I know everybody says that, but it's true." "Ok, he said, it could be true, but what makes you think it's any different now?" "Because the world is going Godless, I answered, and I feel that God is our only salvation."

"You have to believe in the power of the universe Mr. Elliott, au! Warren I mean." "Believing in God, the kingdom of heaven, eternity, and reincarnation for that is the circle of life." "You wonder why most people have forgotten about all these things." "It obvious don't you think, for now we have to fight just to keep the cross on the hill, the nativity set in our own front yards, kids at school can't recite the pledge of legions with the word under God." "It's alright to be Atheist if you want, the Christians won't interfere." "If Atheist doesn't like the cross on the hill, they shouldn't look, if they don't like the nativity set, don't look at that either." "As far as the pledge of legions goes, if their kids don't want to participate, then they can stand in the hall, until those who do have the right to say, under God, have said, under God." "We need God in our world take him out, and we're done for, end of civilization as we know it." "I don't believe we should have to give up our religious rights to please the Atheist, since we are not asking them to give up their rights to believe, they can believe anyway they want to believe." "No one really knows the truth, but we should be free to choose anyway we want to go." "The fact that religion is fading away is a big concern to me." "Am I wrong to feel this way Warren?" "Not at all Darby, he answered, not at all." "I know you must think that just because I'm a psychiatrist, I must be an Atheist." "Let me ease your mind, I'm not, I believe in God, I just believe that when you are dead, your dead, and you stay dead until the resurrection."

"To believe in God, I said, means to believe in life eternal, eternal that means no death, that means we live always and forever, reincarnation is one of these always and forever kind of thing." "We live, the body dies, and we live." "Some go to the light, some hang around here, and some go to a dimension far beyond anyplace we know, these seem to be the lost souls, the souls that need help in finding the light." "Warren these are the souls that seek me out, if they had to wait until the resurrection, how could they be here, how could they come to me for help?" "However it's my belief that the resurrection isn't for the dead, it's for the living." "The dead move on the second they take their last breath."

He seemed to avoid the question that I had just asked altogether, for some reason he didn't want to answer, maybe he thought that his life wasn't the one on the line here, and he brought it right back to me. "You have some very strong views there young lady, so what makes you think taking God out of the world will be the end?" It was starting to look like I had made a big mistake bringing up the Bible, for now it seems that that was going to be the only topic for the day. My views were strong views, and it looked as though we were going to solve those views before getting to the real reason for this visit. "Well it's like this," I said. "If you've read the Bible, that's the way it always ends up, death, and destruction to all when God no longer exist." "I don't know that I believe the Bible to be the complete gospel either, I believe that it was set up as a controlling device, but I know we need to keep God in our world."

"Do you have a plan to keep God in the world Darby?" He asked. "The answer to that would be no, I guess" It seemed like such a dumb question coming from a psychiatrist, so I volunteered an even dumber answer. "I'm not the savior, but I can tell you this; the people of today all believe that the savior will return and save them, so they are waiting for that to happen." "It's not going to happen until they decide to ask him in prayer to come save them." "It was the people of the world that took him out, and it will have to be the people of the world that pray for his return." "Praying and asking is the only way he will feel welcome enough to return." "Should I ask how you know this?" "Spirit Guides give information," was my answer. "It wasn't my Spirit Guide that gave this information, but I read it somewhere, I think it was Earlyne Chaney's Spirit Guide, or some other spiritual being that she had contact with." "And this Earlyne Chaney is who?" He was writing on his note pad again as he was asking questions, so I thought I should wait to answer, but he looked up and said. "Well who is she?" So I told him who I thought she was. "Earlyne Chaney is a writer and teacher of all kind of psychic events, and I believe she is the founder of Astra" "Astra is a spiritual organization based on religion, but more of a new age kind of thing." "Mrs. Chaney has Spirit Guides, but she is a very spiritual person all on her own." "Now the Spirit Guides are telling me that she has passed on to spirit."

This information seemed worthless as none of it was taking us where we needed to go, more or less we were heading down a dead-end road, but he continued with this line of questions, and I continued to answer with the same dead end answers. I couldn't see how any of this was ever going to solve my mental condition. Maybe I would just wind up in a mental institution.

"So I'm to believe that you have a Spirit Guide that talks to you as well, and these Spirit Guides give you information about the future is that right?" "I have a Spirit Guide, I answered, I'm not sure that what he gives me is futuristic, he just helps me to cope with life on this side of the veil, and on the other side as well." "I've told you that he only appears in my dreams, and until now I haven't paid much attention to him, but from now on I plan to hang on to everything he does, and everything he says." "I feel life would be much easier if people realized they were more than a human shell." "See, Warren, I was telling him, when people realize that their body is nothing more than a shell, they can detach from it, and from there the universe is the limit, via Spirit Guides, or out of body travel, or whatever."

The doctor was looking down at his note pad, tapping his pencil now on the edge of his desk. "What if I believe that you only dance on this planet for a short time, and when the music stops, the lights go out, and that's the end of life, or that's the end of life as we know it?" "What would you say to that Darby?" He was looking real serious, and I was thinking he really did believe that life ended with the last breath. I found myself feeling sorry for this man. Suddenly, and without warning, there was a ghostly, womanly figure, which appeared behind his chair, taking me completely by surprise. Where had she come from, and what was she trying to say? Oh! It had to be his mother. That's who she was! I was hearing what she had to say, but I didn't see her mouth moving, that was kind of odd in my opinion. "He was always been a stubborn child," she was saying. "I was hoping someone like you would come along to help him out, he needs a lot of guidance." "Well I'm the one that is supposed to be having therapy here," I said. "Yes you are Darby." "It looks like we are making progress here after all!" Warren was answering as though I had addressed him with that statement. He hadn't heard a word the ghostly figure had said.

I couldn't tell him I thought his dead mother was behind his chair, and that she was talking to me. I was thinking he would never believe it since he didn't believe in the dead. "You're right," the ghost was saying. "He would never believe you!" I hadn't said that out loud, she was picking up on my thoughts. "He thinks life is like a merry-go-round when the ride is over, it's over." "Oh! That's terrible," I said. "No that's good we're making progress, he said, progress is always good." It was like having a two way conversation with a one way receiver, and I knew I shouldn't speak out loud to her again. I was sending her a mental picture letting her know that this was only the first of many sessions to come, and that one, or maybe both of us would be getting the therapy we needed. She was smiling as she disappeared as quickly as she had appeared.

"I need to talk to you about the ghosts I see doctor, if there isn't any life after death, how would you explain a ghost?" "I would explain it as a figment of your imagination, or hallucinations." "Are you on any kind of medication?" "No doctor, I answered, but I see these things anyway." "Some are like shadows, some are like real people, and some are like a thin piece of paper that you can see through." "Then there are those that you know are there, but you don't see them at all." "You know Darby, I'd like to believe that what you are saying is the truth, but it's just a hard concept to swallow." "I believe that you believe, so we'll just say it's a fact." "Is that fair?" "I guess that's fair doctor, but I'm going to tell you about all my ghostly experiences anyway whether you believe me or not." "You do know that is the real reason I'm here?" "It's because of the ghosts, and invisible people, I see and hear that makes me strange to the world of unbelievers."

I started telling him about all the dreams that I had had, hoping that would help him to understand a little about the real me, even though I didn't understand the real me. I had no idea why I could see and hear these things, but I told him they didn't bother me as much as they seemed to bother everybody else. "Haven't you ever had anybody talk to you about the near death experience doctor?" "Call me Warren, Darby, please call me Warren." "The answer to that is no, but I think I'm going to hear about it now, I'm I right?" "Well I don't know Warren, maybe we'll talk about out of body experiences, now I know you've heard about that?" "I've heard people talk about these things, he answered, I've heard you talking about these things, but talking and doing are two different things Darby, and since its only hearsay I'm not quite sure that it exists"

"Warren I'm just going to explain my views, and the differences between the near death experience, and the out of body experience." "I know it sounds a little crazy, but it is totally my idea." "Maybe if you understood my reasoning it would all make a little more sense." "I had a dream once where I was coming down this long tunnel, I knew that you were supposed to go up, not down to get to the light, but I was traveling down, the next thing I remembered was slipping into the body of a new born baby, and that is where the dream ended." "To me it meant that I had left an old life for a new life, and leaving an old life for a new life means reincarnation."

"Since then I have listened and analyzed every story I've ever heard about the near death experience and the out of body experience as well, and I have come to one conclusion." "When people talk about having an out of body experience, they all see a sliver cord." "When people talk about the near death experience, they all talk about a tunnel, seeing their life flash before their eyes, then a light, if they go into the light they know they won't come back." "Those that made it back realize they didn't fully enter into the light." "The theory here then is the sliver cord is the tunnel, it was the way we came into life, and it is the way we well go out." "Like the umbilical cord that feeds the unborn fetus, the silver cord feeds the spirit into the body, everything in your life then is recorded within the sliver cord, so when you travel back through the cord, you see your life flash before your eyes." "It is only a theory Warren, but to me it explains the fact that we do have a life after death." "We come in, and we go out, over and over again. Warren there is life after death, that is what that dream had to mean." "There is reincarnation."

"As you said Darby, it's only a theory, it doesn't prove a thing, and reincarnation is a-far-out theory, wouldn't you agree?" "Absolutely not Warren, I do not agree, I could never agree." "I believe we have lived many lives." "Do you know I have spirits in my house Warren?" He was shaking his head and pushing his pencil through his hair as though he couldn't believe what he was hearing, then he answered "Well you did say your house was haunted, I guess that means you have spirits in your house." "But what is it that makes you think you have spirits in your house, that's what I really want to know?" "I see them, I answered, my friend Charlotte sees them, and my friend Lucy wants to see them but she is too afraid." "Ok, he said, we'll say you have a few ghosts hanging around, we'll just have to see if we can get rid of them." I laughed at his response, as I assured him that it would take a Priest to get rid of them, and since they seemed to be benevolent, there would be no need for a Priest.

"Our time is running out here today Darby, but I can see you again in a week." "We can talk then about that entire unwelcome guest you have, and maybe I will come visit them myself." "I'm open to believing, and I want to believe, believe me!"

The ghostly woman figure appeared behind him once more, she wasn't saying anything just shaking her head in denial, and I knew she wasn't buying his believe me bit for a second. I couldn't say that I was completely convinced either. I was just relieved that he was willing to take it into consideration, so adding a parting comment to his theory of unwanted guest. I voiced my opinion. "I have tried to make my so called unwanted guest feel welcome, Warren, without their visitation I would be almost completely alone, and I really don't want to get rid of them, but I have made a promise to send a couple of them into the light." "When you make promises to ghosts, it's a good idea to keep those promises, wouldn't you agree?"

Now that I was preparing to leave I started to feel a deep sad feeling of despair. I had really felt a strong connection to this man, and now I didn't want this session to end. What it was I couldn't explain. I said good-bye, and made an appointment for the following week. I was wishing the week was over, and that I was just getting here instead of just leaving. There was an unusual heaviness in my chest, and I had a sudden urge to cry. I found away somehow to overcome my feelings and made my way to the parking lot where my big brown Oldsmobile was waiting for me. I don't know how long I sat there, but it had to be quite some time as now the five o'clock traffic was buzzing, and inching my way along the roadway toward home was taking forever.

All the way home I thought about Warren Elliott, he was good looking, he was friendly, and he was fifteen or twenty years younger than me. It wasn't a love connection for I had all the love I needed. I had Jack and Jack was all I would ever need. I loved my husband and my husband loved me. I felt that it had to be because he was listening, and listening with interest. Of course it was his job to listen so giving him credit for that didn't count. Jack always seemed to have something else on his mind, so listening to my tales of ghostly activity wasn't on his priority list.

I couldn't wait until the next morning to tell Lucy all about Warren, and about the ghostly woman that had appeared in his office, so as soon as I got home, I gave her a call asking her over. She was more than a little anxious to find out all the details so I hardly had time to hang up the phone before she was at my door. The tale of the ghostly woman seemed to be most intriguing to her, and I had to explain in detail every move the ghost had made. I had to give a complete description, and Lucy seemed amazed at the fact that even in a Doctor's office, I could come face to face with a ghost. I told her how handsome Warren Elliott was, and how I felt that his good looks were in comparison only to the movie star, Leonardo Dicaperio. He has the same beautiful eyes, eyes as blue as the clear blue sky, I told her, anyway I laughed, blue when we have a clear blue sky.

Jack was also interested in my visit to the psychiatrist office, and wanted to know all about my experience. Of course most of the details for Jack had to be forfeited. There was absolutely no way I could tell him that I enjoyed the doctor's company, or that I was still seeing invisible people, that would only prove to him that I needed additional help. I was trying to prove my normalcy, and proving that I wasn't losing my sanity. If I had mentioned the ghostly apparition, Jack would have thought the therapy had failed. If I had mentioned how good looking the Doctor was then he might think I was having a mid-life-crisis, needing extra care, and looking after. I just wanted to get this psychiatrist thing over with, and move on with my life.

Around noon the next day my son Ken called. He had the pictures developed that he had taken at my birthday party, and in all but one of the photos there were dark shadows in humanly form. First he had thought that the film was flawed, and that what he was seeing couldn't possibly be for real, so he called my son Don, and found out that the pictures he had taken also had shadowy figures, now they were both convinced that I had evil entities invading my home. All I was thinking was, I had proof now for, Jack, for Warren, Lucy, Charlotte, and anybody else who might be thinking I was imaging things. Of course Lucy and Charlotte had always believed in me. Charlotte had even helped me to realize that the shadow people were really heavenly beings. Shadows of heavenly, spiritual entities, so bright, they felt the need to cloak themselves in shadow, to hide their bright spiritual bodies.

Charlotte being a medium knew, I had spirits in my house, she had even been able to communicate with them, but how could I have ever mentioned this to my children. Lucy had accepted the fact that the spirits were there, but she really didn't want to see them. I told Ken they were benevolent, and nothing to worry about, however, I soon learned that it was going to take more than telling him the ghosts were friendly, for even a friendly ghost was more than he could handle. This didn't seem to ease his worried mind knowing that they were friendly either. The next day both Ken and Don were at my door, they brought the photos, and now I had some explaining to do. They were both wondering why I had never told them about all the ghostly activity that had been going on. What could I say? I didn't have an answer, and there was nothing I could say except, that I didn't want to worry them.

Of course both boys had taken double copies of the photos knowing that I would want pictures of the birthday party, and updated pictures of my grandchildren. They knew how proud I was of all my grandchildren, and that I always wanted new photos for my brag book. It was easy enough to notice the shadows in each and every photo. There was a shadow along with each child. While I thought the photos were great, the boys didn't like the exposure their children had gotten from the uninvited guest. However, all I could say to that was, "Chill-out!" "Those uninvited guests haven't hurt anybody."

I had the thought that it would be fun to have the photos enlarged and hung on the wall, then I would have living, and dead proof that the spirit world really did exist. Ken and Don both thought that was a bad idea. They told me that I would just be encouraging the spirits, and they thought of a much better idea. A better idea of course meant that their dad and I should move. Moving wasn't an option for us however, this was the home that Jack and I planned to live in for evermore. My guess was they didn't know how much this place meant to their dad and me. They didn't know that it would take a lot more than a few uninvited spirits to get us to move. I tried explaining to them that all the so-called spirits wanted was help, my help, but that didn't seem to matter. I must have been somewhat convincing however, for when they finally left they were feeling much better about the whole ordeal.

It was the following week that I made plans with Lucy to visit the old homestead of the Warrick's. Before we went, I told Lucy that we might meet Megan, maybe even Tommy there, so if that should happen, and she was unable to see, or hear what was going on, I asked that she give me a signal. The signal was so I could translate whatever they might be saying. Knowing that Jack hadn't been able to see Megan, the possibility of Lucy seeing her was quite slim. She hadn't been able to see Megan the night of the big storm. Lucy was more than pleased to cooperate as the thought of seeing ghosts still scared her more than she wanted to admit. The signal that I asked her to give was to cover her mouth with her right hand, and cough twice.

The biggest problem we were going to have now would be explaining to the occupants living on the property why we were there, and what we had planned for removing any leftover entities, entities that had not yet moved on into the light. We were taking the chance of being run off like a couple of loonies. "What other choices do we have?" Lucy asked. "If we're going to do this we have to go, there's no other way." I knew she was right because Tommy and Megan had to be together, and finding them together at any place other than the Warrick property was a big impossibility.

The drive up the mountainside was a pleasant one. The beautiful scenery unfolded in front of us as we drove. It almost made you wonder why more people hadn't decided to live out here, the air so fresh, the sky so blue, and the smell of the pines so refreshing. The drive to the Warrick property took less than two minutes, and would have only been a short walk, but as anxious as we were to get there, we had decided to drive. What if the new occupants shot at us, we could make a fast get-away, in a fast car.

We had almost talked ourselves out of stopping by the time we got there, but as crazy as all this had to sound, we had to do, what we had to do. We had made the promise to Charlotte, and to Mr. and Mrs. Thornton to send Megan and Tommy into the light. So can you really back out of promises to ghosts? They might haunt you for the rest of your life.

As I made my way to the door of the now beautiful home that sat on the Warrick property, I thought I caught a glimpse of Megan out of the corner of my eye. Lucy was trailing behind me, not saying a word, kind of holding on to my shirttail like a frightened child. We walked up about four steps to the door, and I was looking around for the button to ring the doorbell, but didn't find one, then I noticed a knocker in the middle of the door it was shaped like a skull-and-crossbones. Lucy noticed it at the same time, and let out a muffled yep! "Let's get out of here," she cried. "The Munster's probably live here." "Don't be silly I told her, it's just a knocker."

I raised the little handle and let go, and it set off a set of chimes that vibrated throughout the whole house. I couldn't believe what a noise that thing had made. Lucy all the while was still holding tight, and hiding behind me.

We were both pleasantly surprised when the door opened, and a nice looking young lady greeted us with a smile, and asked us politely to come in. "We don't get much company out here," she was saying, "What is it that I can do for you?" I felt the grip on my shirttail loosen, and I heard Lucy breathe a little sigh of relief. I knew it wasn't going to be an easy task telling her what it was we were really there for, so I just started off by introducing the two of us and telling her we were practically neighbors and thought it was time for a neighborly visit. She in turn introduced herself, and told us that she, and her husband, and two small children had only lived there for about a year. Lucy and I listened with a great deal of interest as she talked about her family and their home life here on the mountain top. She told us her name was Susan Yates, her husband's name was Fred, their children, Annie the little girl was four, and their little boy Joey, was two and a half. She was the first one to mention that there might be something strange going on with their home. She told us that the property had been put on the market and sold numerous times, and that she and her husband would like to do the same. "There are a lot of strange happening going on here she said, that's probably why nobody has lived here for any amount of time."

"Are you planning on moving out?" Lucy asked. It was the first time she had even dared to speak. "We want to Susan answered, but we can't everything we have has been invested in this place." "Nothing real bad has happened here, she said, just doors that open and close by themselves, and the toilet that flushes itself." "Sometimes there are strange noises, and sometimes we have things broken that shouldn't have been." "So far it's just little things that keep happening, but the little happenings still scare us a lot."

The information that Susan had given us about her home was the clue we needed to explain the real reason we were there. Susan's face was turning a little pale as I started explaining to her what we thought was going on. She was ringing her hands, and every so often wiping her brow with a tissue that she had taken for the tissue box that sat on the small inn table in front of us. She was nervous, we could tell, yet she offered with a faint smile to fix us a cup of tea. We declined her offer, but ask if we might look around a little bit. I assured her that if Megan was around I would be able to see her. Susan agreed without hesitation. If there was any way we could find Megan and Tommy, and send them into the light she would be in complete agreement.

The search proved futile however as neither Tommy nor Megan was to be found. We walked around the outside of the house calling out to Megan hoping that she would show herself, but that was not to be, not today. Before we left we gave Susan our telephone numbers, Lucy's and mine, and asked her to call if any of the strange happenings should begin again, and she promised that she would.

As we were preparing to leave Susan followed us to our car. "I just want you to know, she said, that I'm not comfortable having ghosts around my children, and if there is anything you can do to get rid of them it would be greatly appreciated." "We're going to try Susan, I answered, but if we can't we have a friend that can, so don't sell out, and move on us just yet." "These ghosts won't hurt you." We said our good-byes, and thanked her for allowing us to look around. We asked if it would be all right to come back at a later date, telling her that until we had finished the mission we had promised to do, we would probably be bombarded with ghostly activity forever. She gave us an open invitation at that time, which Lucy and I both thought was a very nice gesture.

The short drive back to my house was a silent one neither one of us wanting to admit that we had failed, yet there was a feeling of accomplishment, for we had met the neighbor up the hill, and now we didn't have to feel so leery about returning. She probably would never become someone we would have over each and every morning for coffee, but at least we could acknowledge her in a pleasant way should we meet her on a down town street. The day wasn't a total loss, we shouldn't have expected to run up there throw around a little holy water and have the whole thing resolved.

As we drove into my driveway I noticed the swing in our front yard swaying back and forth. The swing was one that Jack had tied to the tree shortly after moving here. It's for the grandchildren, he had told me, yet both of us had enjoyed a few evening sitting, swinging, and watching the wild life that ventured in through the open fields. It was just the swing moving back and forth, the wind wasn't blowing, and then suddenly there was Megan.

I was yelling, "Oh! Lucy look there's Megan, she's in the swing can you see her?" "No, no! Darby, I can't," she answered. "We have to talk to her, so forget about your signal, it's alright if you can't see her, I'll translate for you." "Come on let's go." "Wait Darby, Lucy said nervously. Do you think this is a good idea?" "This is a very good idea Lucy." I was assuring her." "Megan is completely harmless, come on."

It only took Lucy enough time to exit the car and run around behind me, for me to feel the grip on my shirttail once again. "Lucy, she's not going to hurt you, so please don't be afraid." "Let's just go," I was practically dragging Lucy as we were inching our way closer to Megan. Megan seemed to drag her feet, and stop the swing momentarily. "I saw you today she said, you came to visit." "That's right Megan" I replied. Why didn't you come out and talk to us." "Lucy she saw us, she knew we were there." I was translating hoping Lucy would feel more at ease, however it only seemed to frighten her a little more, for now she was scrunching in behind me closer than before.

"Tommy is afraid of all the people in our home, she was saying, he was afraid of you." "Megan will you stop the swing, I asked, I can't talk to you when you're going back and forth, back and forth." All of a sudden the swing stopped, it had swung backwards and stopped in mid-air that in its self would have been frightening to a normal person because there was nothing holding it there. Her feet hadn't touched the ground. There was no dragging of the feet, absolutely nothing, just a sudden stop. She was sitting there looking down at the ground, the swing still back, and up on the back swing. It would have appeared that someone was behind her, holding her from coming down. As calmly as I could, I asked her to bring the swing down, and at that moment it slowly started to drop kind of like hitting the space bar on a typewriter one inch at a time.

"Megan, I said, the house you think is yours and Tommy's is not yours anymore, you and Tommy are both deceased." "You both died in a fire that destroyed the Warrick's home many years ago." "The people that are living there now are the ones that are supposed to be there." I didn't have time to tell her anything else because she dissolved instantly right before my eyes. Megan had never vanished like that before, and I was wondering if I had gotten through to her, or if what I had just told her was so unbelievable that she didn't want to talk anymore. I was beginning to think it was the latter, and vanishing was her only escape. I had frightened her so badly that she may never materialize again.

"She's gone Lucy, I said, I guess I shouldn't have told her that way now she is in a disbelieving mode, and now it's going to be harder to get through to her." "Did you see the swing stop in mid-air? I asked Lucy. "I didn't see anything Lucy answered. "The swing didn't move at all, it's still sitting as it was before." It was then that I realized that Megan wasn't seeing into my dimension, but me seeing into hers. "Do you think she will tell Tommy? Lucy asked. "I don't know I answered, but I'm sure that whatever happens we will really have to work a lot harder at it now." "Well should we go back again tomorrow? Lucy asked. "No Lucy," I was telling her, there was no way I could go back tomorrow, because my appointment with Warren Elliott was scheduled for that day. "Oh! I see, she said, you've got to go see your boyfriend." "Lucy!" I was shocked that she would say such a thing. "He isn't my boyfriend, he's just a shrink, and you know I need shrinking." "Anyway, I said, he is much too young for me, he's more your age." "Well Lucy replied, "Steve is all the man I can handle, so I'll just have to pass on that one."

It was good that we could still laugh and joke after all that had happened, and even though it was now past noon, we decided we needed another pot of coffee. Lucy had left her children with her mother-in-law much to long for one day, and she was feeling a little guilty, but not guilty enough to say no to coffee, so we soon found ourselves setting drinking coffee, and eating grilled cheese sandwiches, super-duper easy to fix on my new waffle grill.

This was a great life Lucy, and I had established for ourselves, we were becoming the ghost busters of Pine Hill Mountain, sharing all our little secrets, and working close together to send all the homeless ghosts off into the light. This was just something we had to do, and thinking of what we had to do, we knew we had to think of Megan. Thinking Megan and her boyfriend Tommy definitely needed to be sent into the light. We wanted to believe we could do this without Charlotte. We wanted to believe we could do this all by ourselves, but Charlotte was an asset we couldn't ignore. Her gift of spirituality surpassed anything Lucy, and I was capable of doing. Charlotte was always busy, she was booked three months in advance with clients, but then Megan and Tommy had been hanging around for twenty eight years, what's another three or four months? It was just that Lucy, and I was impatient, and wanted everything to happen now.

I had more pressing issues at hand now anyway! I couldn't be thinking of Megan, I couldn't be thinking of Tommy, or any other stubborn entities that might be roaming the planet. I had an appointment with my shrink, and just like the first visit, I was nervous as hell. I wanted to see Warren, but at the same time, I didn't want to see Warren, because he only agitated my total being.

He made me feel that my whole life had been a lie, and that what I was seeing, and hearing couldn't be for real, making me feel like a wild-ass dreamer. Maybe my dreams did seem wild and unearthly, but unearthly or not, it was my reality, and one thing everyone has to remember, reality is whatever you yourself make of it. It's that thing called freewill. However you have to know that by using your freewill you are only activating your own thoughts! Everything that ever was, started from a single thought, including your freewill. I use to believe my thoughts were private, and it took a long time for me to realize that thoughts were things. So the old saying be careful of what you wish for, you might get, is for real. Think about it!

Tomorrow is the day for me, I'm off to see the shrink, and I'll not be following the yellow brick road. Tumbling out of bed there was no dream, so no writing in my dream genie. I shut off the alarm clock, woke Jack, and headed off to the kitchen to make coffee, and breakfast. After Jacks morning ritual and my usual morning goodbye kiss, I started my shower. Then what seemed like hours I was finally ready for my next vitiation with my psychiatrist.

CHAPTER FIVE

The second visit started out a little differently than the first, this time, Warren had to know all my family background. He wanted to know how many members of my family were still living, and how many of them were deceased, what they did for a living when they were alive, and basically what kind of people they were. Of course all he truly wanted to know was whether or not I came from a dysfunctional family. It was only my parents, and my siblings that he wanted to know about, so the long dive into my long lost past began.

"We were a family of seven, mother, father, two brothers, two sisters, and myself, and now there are two, my younger sister, Holly and me." "My youngest brother died at age three, my oldest sister died at age twenty four, my older brother just recently at age fifty. My father died three years before my mother, and at the time of their death, they had both reached the old age of eighty." "Now what is it you want to know about them, Warren?" "What were they like, and did you have any problems with them as you were growing up?" "Did any of your family members claim to be psychic?" "No I answered, I was the only oddball in the family, and there weren't any problems." "Can we move on from here?" "Most of my relatives are dead and gone now." "Now there are more grave markers than living relatives, and I really don't like talking about that." "Finding out about your childhood is half the battle you know, he said, so we'll talk about that later."

"Well! I said, my older sister may have had some psychic ability." "Long before I was able to see spirits my older sister would tell me about the man in white that came at night, he had four white dogs, and he had them doing tricks for her." She would ask me if I could see them, and when I said no, she would tell me what they were doing. Jumping through hoops, rolling a ball, going up a flight of stairs, standing on their back legs, or just whatever it was they might be doing. It was at that time in my life that my little brother and I were having a time in the astral dimensions as well. When I'd fall asleep he would come for me, and we would spend our dreams together in wonderland. There was no way to describe the beauty, the joy, and the pleasure these experiences had on me, and talking about them now makes me shudder, and leaves me a little breathless. At the age of five, my little brother was the best thing going in my life, I loved him so"

Your little brother seems to be the trigger to the bigger problem in your life, a bigger problem than all the rest, why do you think that is Darby?" "I don't know I answered, there hasn't been a day in the past forty three years I haven't thought about him, forty three years he's been gone, and I still think of him every day." "It isn't that I loved him more it's, just that was my first experience with death, and I did love him, I didn't want to lose him, but I loved my other brother, sister, mother, and father as well, and as much" "I've come to a better understanding of death now and can except their passing with more compassion, and I feel grateful that they are in a better place than we are." "I have Holly, the one sister left in this dimension, and I love her too."

"I have to stop thinking about the past now because I have a wonderful family of my own." "I have a daughter with two puppy dogs, two sons, and five grandchildren." "I also have two wonderful daughter-in-laws." What more could any mother ask for, I had it all.

Of course he wanted to know about my three children, and five grandchildren, but what could I say they were all normal. I wasn't having any problems with my marriage so that wiped out most of his strategy on question asking. That's when the conversation went from therapy to casual anything goes conversation. We started talking about dreams.

My wild dreams were one topic that seemed to interest Warren, so that's where we spent an endless amount of time. We were discussing the unrealistic dreams of flight, and all the dreams that seemed to be more down to earth, meaning anything that didn't require a skating party into the wild beyond. He seemed to think that if he could understand my dreams, he could understand my problems. I was telling him that almost everything came to me in the world of dreams, and if the problem couldn't be solved in the waking hours of the day, then all I had to do was go to sleep, and the whole scenario would unfold. One dream that I especially liked was when I lived a life on another planet. The planet had two suns, they seemed to be the same distends away, and the same size as our moon, they were side by side. The rising suns were from the west, and the settings were in the east. It was a peaceful planet, and why I chose to be reincarnated on this planet was more than I could understand.

"Reincarnation" he said. "There's that word again." "Why do you still believe in reincarnation?" "Why is that? He asked. "We've had this conversation before, I answered, and I believe it because it's real." "When you dream, Warren I said, everything you want to know about in life, about your past life, or your future life, it's all there, all you have to do is pay attention." "Warren, I said, even you, when you go to bed at night tell yourself I'm going to remember my dreams, and as soon as you wake up write down everything that you can remember." "After a while you will find that you can ask for answers to any problem, and then while you sleep the answers will come to you." "Then I guess I'm going to ask my dream genie how to understand my complicated patient." He was grinning as he spoke, and I knew he was not taking me serious at all.

His theory on reincarnation was what fascinated me the most, so I really have to tell you about that. It started with him talking about the scientist developing a technology for the purpose of down loading memory from one brain to another so as the first person would live forever. "That's reincarnation" he said. I didn't mean to laugh at his theory, yet, I knew that a psychiatrist believed more in science than they did in religion and my snickering seemed unnerving to him as now he was asking me; "What do you think about that, Darby?" Not wanting to seem disrespectful, as I knew he was entitled to his opinion. I asked him a question instead. "What if you down loaded your memory right now while you are still a live Warren? I asked. "Wouldn't you have to say that was cloning?" "If the technology didn't replace the individual then you have done nothing more than made a copy, one real and one a lie." "I couldn't say unreal because both would be a real person, both believing they were the original." "It's like recording a movie on a VCR tape, the original movie stays the same, and the new movie is the same unless you decide to change or add to it." "All you've managed to do is give false memories to a new body that you will never live in" "So each movie, the old and the new, goes on to make memories of their own there ever after." "That's not reincarnation, that's cloning, or copying, but definitely not reincarnation."

"The problem with scientist, I was telling him, was that they all seemed to think they can create anything that God can create." "This reminds me of a joke," I told him." "Do you what to hear it." He laughed a little, but he said, "Oh, alright it's your dime if you want to waste it by telling jokes go ahead." "Well it's like this" I said. "The scientist and God were arguing over the fact that they could each create man, so God said to the scientist, I'll create man then you can show me how you can create man, and the scientist agreed, so God reached down picked up a hand full of dirt, and created man. The scientist then reached down to the ground, and picked up a hand full of dirt, and as he did so, he heard a big loud voice saying, "Oh! No you don't, get your own dirt." "The morel to this story is no matter how smart the scientist thinks he is, he still has to use material that has already been created." "We only have one God, and he doesn't claim to be a scientist."

"I read somewhere were the speech of the Dolphin was a form of English, it was just so loud, and so fast that it was unrecognizable, whenever it was slowed down, and I mean way down, you could actually understand what was being said." "I use to believe that in the days of Atlantis there may have been some down loading of memory into four or five, or a few dozen Dolphins, and as smart as they were they may have passed the language on to their young."

"Of course I know the truth now." "They are the oldest living species living on our planet today, also one of the most intelligent species living on our planet today." "Through astral-travel, I have learned that the Dolphin was an implant from a different planet." "I was told that their planet was dyeing due to their sun burning out, and going dark." "It was believed that they would be safe here." "They had large oceans that were pure until mankind polluted the water." "I was told this, via my guides." "However, my belief system was a little off here, according to my Spirit Guides." "My guides said I was just being a little judgmental of the scientist who weren't trying to play God with an act of cloning Dolphins, but they would if they could." "A different planet for survival would be required now if the Dolphins were to continue to survive, neither Astrologers, nor Scientist have a clue." "They prefer only to clone, their way of Reincarnation or playing God."

"You don't have much respect for the scientist do you?" Warren asked. "Of course I do," I answered. "I just don't believe that they should try to take over the role of God." "They may be able to create a body, but can they create a soul?" "If the clone has a soul it is because it was in the DNA of the material used." "And you've learned this through your dream therapy, I suppose, or your Spirit

Guides, am I right?" "You can make fun of my dream therapy if you want to Warren, and you can make fun of my Spirit Guides, but you shouldn't knock the experience until you've tried it."

"Well let's see has there been any ghostly activity in your life since I've seen you last?" Warren was changing the subject. I was guessing that the scientist issue was getting to hot for him to handle. All the while I was eager to tell him about Megan, not that he would believe me, but just because it was such a fascinating tale to tell. He listened as I told him how the swing had stopped in mid-air, and how she had vanished into thin air. I was waiting for his response, but there was nothing, just a look of wow me with another one. So if that wasn't enough for his attention then I was capable of digging a little deeper.

"I have photos," I was telling him, and at the same time, I was reaching for my purse, digging for the ghostly pictures. If the photos of shadow people weren't enough to convince him of ghostly activity, then I knew, there would be no hope at all. I scattered the pictures out on his desk, and waited for his response. Just as I had thought, a doubting look came across his face, and he began to shake his head. "This is nothing, nothing at all!" "Just poor lighting, could be they are shadows of whoever was taking the picture." "Can't you believe anything other than your science book Warren?" I was a little baffled at his disbelief. "You've got to be a little more open minded, I was telling him, especially if you are ever going to understand me." "It's life, its death, it's the living after living," "There's more to life Warren than scientific research." "Here I thought I had proof, substantial evidence beyond a shadow of a doubt, no pun intended, but I thought my shadow people photos were quite convincing." "What is it going to take to prove to you that life is everlasting?" "You know Darby, he said, convincing me is not the proof in the pudding, no pun intended, it's you this therapy was scheduled for." "What I believe, or what I don't believe, is irrelevant." "Ok, I said, so as not to make the good doctor mad, crazy, or insane, maybe we should stick to dreaming."

"Dreaming is good, he said. Your dreams are interesting, different but interesting."

It was at that time that I actually did start to dream. I don't know if you can call it remote viewing, out of body travel, or simply disconnect from reality, but I was paying no attention to the good Doctor anymore. It seemed that whenever I wanted to escape form the situation at hand I simply drifted away. The thought of him ever believing in the supernatural was a dream. If he couldn't believe a little bit then how, I was thinking, was he ever going to believe in me. I guess I knew from the first visit that I was wasting my time, and his. If it wasn't for Jack who wanted this therapy for me I would just walk out, and never return, but Jack being so skeptical on the supernatural, believed that help was only a psychiatrist away.

Disappointing Jack the man I loved so much wasn't anything I could ever do, and I was thinking of Jack at that moment. "Darby, Darby, where did you go?" I was being summoned back. "Oh! I'm sorry I said, I guess I took a leave of absents there for a minute or two." "Well that's ok, he told me, it's just that our time is running out here, and we're still entangled in a few misconceptions." "We'll work on more dreams, and dream genies on your next visit, so please make your appointment on the way out." "I'll see you soon."

I wanted to say no I'm not coming back, not next week, not ever, but I didn't do that, I stopped made my appointment with June his receptionist, and told her the succession went well, and that I'd see her next week. I wasn't thinking it went well at all, as a matter of fact, I was feeling depressed. The feeling was anger maybe, almost all the people on the planet had come to the realization that reincarnation was a for real deal, God had been into recycling forever. Then there was Warren, the one person I needed to believe, still being a holdout.

I had more things to think about other than Warren Elliott, I had shopping to do for tomorrow night was the night for the real ghosts and goblins to appear. Halloween, spooky night, bewitching night, the night I was sure Lucy would want to find out more of the tricks I had up my sleeve. The only trick-or-treaters I would get would be the ten little tricksters from next door, and maybe even the two from up the hill, but I had to have special treats for all just the same, so with ten plus two little plastic pumpkins filled to the brim with all kinds of candy, I headed for home.

Lucy was going to be disappointed that I didn't have one unusual thing to tell her concerning Warren Elliott. There was not one unusual thing, no ghostly activity, nothing remotely interesting about Warren Elliott, nothing to speak about, nothing. As soon as she saw me pull into my garage, she was on her way over. "Well how did it go?' She asked. "Not well, not well at all." I answered. "Will you help me carry in this candy please?" "Wow!" "Why so much candy?" "I'm expecting a few little goblins tomorrow night." I told her. "You know the night the dead comes alive." "Haw, she laughed, that's every night at you house." "Awe--right, but at midnight on Halloween, they are in every nook and cranny." "You don't have to have any special potions, or broom sticks to sweep them out, they just come out, and get you." "Well Lucy said, since nothing unusual happened today maybe we can make something unusual happen tomorrow night, maybe at midnight after the kids have gone to bed." "I'll bring them over early for trick-or-treat, then Steve can take the older ones to town somewhere." "Margie can put the little ones to bed, and I can come over." I had to laugh at Lucy, she always wanted something to happen, even though I knew she would be scared completely out of her wits, should that actually happen.

"How about your Ouija board Darby, could we use the Ouija board tomorrow night?" "Lucy you know we can use the Ouija board, I answered, but it's so slow." "I thought we had agreed never to do that again" "When we use the board the messages come through one letter at a time, do you really want to do that?" "I talk to the dead Lucy, I don't need a Ouija board to talk to the spirit world, their messages come through loud and clear." "I can tell you what they are saying in a matter of minutes." "Well great then, she answered, I guess you're right!" "Can we do that, can we?" "Tomorrow night I answered, midnight be here."

After carrying in all the candy Lucy and I settled down for our afternoon delight, a stemming cup of hot chocolate, topped with marshmallows severed before the fire that was now blazing in the fireplace. "This would be so romantic, Lucy said, if only Jack and Steve were here." I had to laugh knowing that Jack and Steve were two of the busiest men in the county, and the thought of them setting in front of a romantic fire place drinking hot chocolate with two psycho women, was a scene that was not likely to come full circle.

"When Jack gets home, I told her, he will have to hose down his little make shift skating rink." "All my kids will be out this weekend to go ice skating." "Oh! That sounds like fun." "Do you skate?" She asked. "If you can call it that, I answered, I go round, and round, but I stay very close to the railing, I'm not as agile as the kids." "You should see them skate." "They do all the fancy little tricks." "Jumping and twisting going round and round on one skate, a double axial they call it." "Oh! Skating backwards now that's a trick." "If I could skate like that it would be like heaven." I was thinking heaven because in my dimensional dreams skating was so easy. I could actually do all the fancy tricks, all the tricks the kids could do, and more. It was just this dimension where the ice was trickier, and harder, the greatest trick was standing upright. "All the winter holidays the kids come out to skate, and play in the snow," I told her. "But since we haven't had any snow yet this year they will just have to settle for skating."

The phone started ringing off the hook at that time. Our visit for the evening was now over, as the caller was none other than Lucy's Mormon husband Steve. His Mormon manly need for a warm womanly body was beckoning her home. What a nerd Steve had to be, I thought, as I watched her slip on her coat, preparing to rush out, run over, and take care of his lusting manhood. The manly, lustful, manhood, that believed that a larger family was now in order. Oh well, as they say the fun is in the trying, so good luck with that one. We know don't we, Lucy Spencer, AKA Sarah Randall.

"Okay! Lucy, see you in the morning, coffee at seven." "I'll be here, don't eat all that candy." "Not on your life girl, I answered, that's just for making the kids nauseated." "Thanks a lot," she called, as she vanished out the door.

Alone again, I thought, maybe a good book would be worthy of my companionship. Jack had informed me that tonight would be one of his late night excursions at the hospital. I was beginning to think the hospital was his mistress, yet I knew being on call until five a.m. meant that a twenty mile drive was much too far should there be a dire emergency. "Not tonight honey he had said, I'll be home by ten." "I'm not staying the night, I promise ten o'clock." "Love you, see you then." Oh! Well, whatever I was totally used to it, and I had my late night talk show to keep me company. Mr. Art Bell, or George Noory, two fantastic talk show hosts, on Coast-to-Coast what a program, I loved every minute of it. Well Jack had his mistress, and I had mine. Maybe my mistresses and I would never meet face to face, but then the hospital couldn't offer much more than that either.

Of course the book I chose to read was James Van Praagh. The title Talking to Heaven, what more could anyone ask for? Here I was in my dimensional fantasyland reading form a book about Heaven, written by a man that was truly connected, and truly believed as I did. The problem was the stillness of the night, with only the warmth, and crackling of the fire in the fireplace. Soon the stillness found me sound asleep. Oh! But fear not for this is where the fun begins. Just like Megan in the swing, I was up in the air, and a hand was reaching for mine. Then as usual I was skating as all professionals do on a beautiful sparkling field of ice. Beautiful sparkling skates on my feet all cares and wows left far behind as the distant horizon closed in and we were ready to step from the ice into the next dimension.

If only I could take everybody on this journey what a total blessing that would be, for being there is the most unbelievable experience imaginable. Reading about it in a dream genie couldn't possibly describe the beauty, the peace, the love, the glory of God, felt as in the travel itself. That's not going to stop me from trying to convey my message to the whole wide world. Maybe entities of the world aren't ready to believe in out-of-body travel, but if only I could find a way to let them know how real it is, then maybe just maybe, there would be more peace than war.

Here, and out-of-body, we were ready to take a few uncharted baby steps into wonderland where beautiful fields of pure gold rolled out like a magic carpet in front of us. Beautiful flowers that seemingly popped up just to say hello, where have you been? We've missed you, welcome back. Leaving me puzzled, welcome back, where have you been, I don't know! Have I been here before? You didn't have to ask, you didn't have to say a word, every thought was an automatic transformation. This was good for there was a great number of thoughts, and a great number of questions all around, however all thoughts, and questions were sorted, not a single one intertwined, or interfered with the other. This was so fascinating. It was the equivalent of down loading a whole encyclopedia instantly. What a fascinating trip!

CHAPTER SIX

My guide was leading me down this magnificent glorious path, true we didn't have to walk. Our magical wings of thought could have transported us anywhere we wanted to go. We could have just thought about where we wanted to go, and wall- la, we would have been there, but sometimes you have to take your time, and take in the whole picture in order to understand the meaning. As we walked I notice animals that on the earthly dimension would have had you for lunch, but here they were as tame as a new born baby kitten. Life here was respected. Everything that had the smallest spark of life was regarded respectfully. The animals taking great care not to step on the smallest of all small plant life, or even the smallest of insects, truly they were showing greater courage than their beastly animal instincts. Animal instincts, on planet earth, or earth's realm per-say, would have been over ruled. They seemed to understand how precious the tiniest of the tiniest sparks of life truly were, and they honored, and respected that tiny life graciously.

We could see the ocean straight ahead of us. Beautiful clear blue water that seemed ever so gently to be lapping at the white sands of the beach, but still we walked in silence. Feeling all the glory that surrounded us, taking in and remembering how powerful the universe was. My subconscious mind was on a rampage as I breathed in, and observed the magnificent paradise unfolding in front of us. With each step we took we saw the different colors popping up enfolding into the scenery, beautiful reds, greens, and blues like none we had ever seen before. The ocean seemed to be taking on a velvet hue, sending a purple mist around the foaming waves. If life on dimension earth could be this peaceful, this serene, and this beautiful, never would there be any heart-ache, pain or suffering. Oh! What a pity, I was thinking! What a pity, what a waste! For earth energy was wasted on greed and power, without the realization that thoughts could have turned earth's realm into a trusting, loving, never ending paradise.

This time at the ocean edge we didn't walk the beach. We simply walked straight into the water, calming, and blue once again, the ocean waves caressing my bare feet, sending warm sensations all through the entirety of my body. To my surprise it wasn't cold like the waters of the Oregon Coast might have been, but rather refreshingly warm, like afresh tub of bath water. I was so taken in with this strange phenomenal experience that I hadn't noticed the Dolphins that where gathering at my feet. There were six maybe seven of the gorgeous little creatures splashing about trying to get my attention. Finally through mental telepathy, I heard their command to sit myself down. The water was waist deep after following their command, and sitting down, but ever so pleasant. I worried about the beautiful gown I was wearing, a multiple colored beautiful full-length red gown that changed from red to different shades of pink and burgundy then back again. Would the water ruin it? Sparkling in the sun light like a fairy princess, all I needed to complete the ensemble was my magic wand.

Worry, worry, I heard again, I was given the message not to worry, everything here was perfect, and worry was not a part of anything in this dimension. I was communicating with the Dolphins, and as I had suspected, they were the intelligent species that I had believed them to be, they seemed to know my every thought. They would lay their beak duck like heads on my lap, and look at me with love, and understanding. In this dimension, understanding was something I was finding hard to do. What was all of this about? Why was I here? What was the purpose of all of this?

My guide was sitting by my side, and smiling ever so pleasantly, he was going to answer all these questions, but not right away, he wanted me to enjoy, and feel the love, and excitement this side of the veil had to offer. So for what seemed like hours we played with the Dolphins, watched the other fish and sea life that played in the warm water. Oh! It's not warm to them, I was told! The ocean conforms to the needs of whatever creature inhabits its waters. Shocked to think the ocean could actually be cold to one, and warm to another, was a reminder of an old nursery rhyme, some like it hot, some like it cold, some like in the pot nine days old. Do you suppose that we all get our inspirations form the other side of the veil? Do we get all these inspirations, speculations, wonderings, and dreams from the heavenly realm? Inspirations sent from heaven to confront all of our wildest dreams, and imagination. Surly truth is the true existence of the never-ending universe.

I was so curious, I still wanted to know why me? The explanation almost made me cry. "Life, all life, no matter how tiny it might be has a purpose." "One spark of life, can affect yet another spark of life, and set into motion the bigger plan." "No one knows what their spark can do to affect the bigger plan, planned for them." "You, he said, your plan would affect the lives of many, and you were meant to be a spokesperson to bring truth to the world." "But I don't know the truth!" I answered. My voice sounded overly concerned even to me as it echoed in my ears. "Why me, that was the question, why me?" "Not to worry, he answered, that's why you're here." "But, but, I said, there's only me, my cat, and my neighbor Lucy. That's not a very big world to preach too." I was still over whelmed, and it definitively resonated in my voice, but I could see the patience and love emanating, engulfing his glowing essences. What a beautiful sight to behold. Mentally I was being shown, and given the message that it wasn't a preaching job. My job, my only job, was to decipher the meaning, and to stay on course. To me it just meant more confusion. I had no idea how to stay on a course, I had no idea I was on.

Whatever was I going to do, maybe ask those brilliant Dolphins? That thought roared in my mind as I thought about running, and splashing farther back, deeper into the warmth of ocean's sparkling security blanket. Here in this dimension, I was completely free, a wonderer, a time traveler, a visitor into the world of Oz. No Darby, I told myself just pay attention, pay attention to the gloriousness of all things going on here. Whatever it is that's going on in this dimension, it's definitely not Oz. We don't have any flying monkeys, or witches dropping houses on our heads, just respect for all living things, like for instants the animals that sidestep the tiny little insects. Life never ends here, so stepping on them would mean nothing at all. It's just the courteous, respectable thing to do.

My brain was bubbling over with denial, even if I had the truth, how could I pass it on, how could I do it? Why, I wanted to know, why me? "Why not you, you're the chosen one Darby?" That's what I was hearing, it was like a recording in my head, and it was coming in loud and clear. Where was that coming from? Oh! Of course my ever knowing, all knowing Spirit Guide. "Let me tell you a little story." My guide said. "A long time ago when you were five years old, you prayed to God." "Do you remember?" "Yes I do," I answered. Now the emotions were building up, and the tears started rolling down my checks. Even in this land of milk and honey, the mention of my long lost baby brother Adrian, brought a floodgate of pain, and sorrow. It was a mystery even to me after all these decades of worldly time that his memory could still haunt me as it did.

"Well not many five year old children pray to God with such a heartfelt request." He was saying. "It was a request that warranted a reply." "You have waited a long time, but you are about to realize that God is real, and that God answers prayers." "It's not an answer to a prayer that you can keep, but a healing to a pray offered up some forty-three years ago." Of course I was thinking, fourth three years, that's right, Adrian had been gone fourth three years, and still just the mention of that tragedy brought over whelming grief, but an answer to a prayer, whatever could he be talking about?

I still didn't understand. It was like nonsense going through my head. Whatever was he talking about? I didn't know, but he wasn't finished. "You've got to know that if you touch the life of one person; that person in return touches the life of someone else, and the ball starts to roll." "Even your ghost friends have a purpose, maybe they don't know, but as you help them, they help you." All of this was far beyond my comprehension. I just didn't know where he wanted me to take this information. "I just do, what I do, because it's what I've always done." I said. "I can't save the world." "That's right!" "We are not asking you to do that, just remember that Adrian was one of those sparks in your life, a spark he had a purpose for, and when he fulfilled his purpose, he then left you, to return to his heavenly home." There was a spark of knowledge, and a spark of spirituality, which he could give, and he gave that to you freely." "That spark is still very much alive, and still rolling through your subconscious mind."

Wow! I had never thought of Adrian as being a spark before, I never thought of him as being knowledgeable, or spiritual, or anything other than Adrian my little brother. I know now that he must have had some kind of spiritual pull in order to roam around at night outside of his crippled little body, but did he really sacrifice himself and his life for me.

That was a horrible thought! I would never want anyone to make such a sacrifice especially my wonderful baby brother, and what does his sacrifice have to do with me saving the world. I was asking, desperately pleading for answers, answers that wasn't about to be revealed, on this astral flight of dreams.

"Well the world maybe a broad statement, he was saying, you can't save the whole world, but you can save a few, and the few you save, can save a few more." "You think you're not important because you live on a mountain top isolated from the outside world, but that's not true. You meet new people, just pay attention and soon the meaning will clarify."

Unreal! Sometimes the answers need more clarifying than the questions. "You make as much sense as my physiatrist, I said." With that a smile came across his face larger than I had ever seen him smile before. "Somebody maybe to help, he said, somebody maybe to help you." "That's right, I said, this guy needs a lot of help. He's more like a scientist than a spiritualist, or even the physiatrist he claims to be." "Just wait until I tell him about this trip, he is going to freak-out." "Well there is a trip that you will be telling him about that is going to freak him out even more, but that is yet to come."

From that remark I was guessing that this wasn't going to be the end of my traveling to far off different dimensions. I was totally happy about that, because this was such a pleasurable journey, I could stand a few more trips like this one. You didn't have to pay airfare, or worry about lost luggage, and the wardrobe now that was something to marvel at.

The Dolphins were doing little flip flops now, and showing off their ability to entertain. They wanted so much to make us feel welcome in our little pool of warm water. As I watched---well---I was thinking of my sister Barbara now. "Can't you see the white dogs?" She would say. "They are doing tricks for us." "No Barbara, I didn't see the white dogs, but I do see the Dolphins, and maybe this is one of those times one life surly does touch another." I definitely felt it was a special touch helping me to remember my older sister Barbara. Many years had passed since Barbara had left earth for the heavenly realm, at that time she was a beautiful young lady, only twenty-four. Twenty-four, and even now in this dimension of love, I remembered, and felt the sadness. The Dolphins seemed to be bringing it all back. They were bringing back the memories of a lost childhood that I had suppressed in order to subdue the pain of loss.

It's alright to feel the sadness, I was being told, because it doesn't last forever. One day all the loved ones in your life will be together again. "Barbara, Adrian, your mother, and father, and your other brother what was his name?" "Cleo!" I answered I thought you knew all that." He was smiling again as he answered me. "We do, he said, but it helps you to speak the names. It helps the grieving process. One day there will be no more sadness, only peace, love and happiness. There will be a blissful reunion where all the souls, you've ever known, in all your life times, will be present." "Hey! I said you're talking reincarnations aren't you?" "I know you believe in reincarnation Darby, so why do you seem so surprised?" I couldn't answer that. It seemed all I could do was shrug my shoulders in surprise. "Before that time comes, he was saying, there is much work to be done." "Much work where you my dear Darby, shall have a life time in witch to do it in."

Well maybe half a lifetime, I thought, I've lived pretty much half already. I've raised three wonderful children, and I've watched my children raise children. These children are going to want their ice skating rink ready, and waiting when they show up this weekend to visit, and skate, mostly skate. Oh! How they loved the little makeshift ice skating rink, Jack, Dad, Grandpa, had made for them.

Thinking about my earthly life was probably preparing me for a quick return to the farm. I had often joked about out-of body experiences as a way to take a trip, and not leave the farm, but I knew it wasn't true. I was totally, and completely gone whenever these trips decided to take me away. I had definitely left the farm, totally unattached from my sleeping body, and earthly responsibilities. My sleeping body stays, I go, and my sanity seemingly gone too for that matter.

Sitting here in the warm water, I could see the sun and it seemed to be going down for it was closing in on the ocean waves. "How wonderful, I said, as I watched in awe. The sun actually sets here." Then I heard a little chuckle from my guide; "No, he said, it's just like the ocean, you thought about the setting sun, and now the sun is setting, but only for you." But how could that be, I wanted to know. "Do you remember the show Oh God?" He asked. "Yes I remember that show." "Do you watch shows here?" "We know all that goes on, he answered, even if it's just a show." "The point, he said is, when John Denver wanted a miracle, God made it rain inside his car." "Why ruin it for everyone." "It's the same here, why ruin it for everyone." "The Dolphins for example, one might want darkness, the one beside him still wanting to enjoy the beautiful sun, so each is granted their desire."

"You say desire instead of wish, why is that?" He seemed to be amused at my silly questions, but he was prepared to answer just the same. "Because wishing isn't a thing anyone has to do here." "It's all in the desire, and all in the thoughts, the thoughts that produce the results, and never does anyone have to say I wish, for all that is necessary is their desire." "The earth dimension at one time was capable of all the same feats, however this provided very little to those who wanted complete control, and soon the greed of those who wanted full rule, and control took precedence over the whole dimension, and the results are what you see." "Is there any way we can change that, and bring our dimension back to its natural state." "No, he answered, I'm afraid that is one boomerang, you'll have to call a stick."

As he spoke he seemed to sparkle, I don't know if it was his aura, or just what it was but, little sparks of blue and gold flashed all around him, rainbows of color formed around his head, and a feeling of trust flowed outwardly into the ocean, like the ocean waves themselves. The Dolphins where swimming closer and closer as though they couldn't get enough of the energy, the compelling essence of a Spiritual Spirit Guide. It would be nice to pocket all this, and take it back whenever the time came for me to return to my body, but there would be no way to convince the doubting Tomas's that a world so perfect existed. Now I wondered what the plan was the plan that I was supposed to follow, in order to make a difference in the world. What spark was I supposed to spark, to set in motion, the next spark that could possibly make that difference?

He was telling me it's like the sands of the beach take away one grain of sand then another until there is nothing left, and you have no beach it's just barren ground. Each grain has a purpose to fulfill, and each grain is there to fulfill that purpose. It's the same with people, and I'm sure, he said, you will find yours.

If this place wasn't so peaceful, I'd probably be running away screaming. I'd always felt that my life had no purpose. Wife and mother was all that was ever to come of it, and I'm finding now that if I ever wanted to step foot into this dimension to stay, (which was a pretty cool thought) I'd have to do something quite spectacular. Getting a clue or a heads up wasn't going to be pointed out either. So now I'm guessing it's back to the drawing board for me.

I wanted to know his name, I was so tired of calling him my guide, and I thought maybe, just maybe he'd tell me now, if I asked. He was way ahead of me, he knew exactly what I was going to ask, but he waited patiently until I found the courage. "What is your name I asked?" A pleasant smile came across his face, and again the sparkles emanated his surroundings. "My name is Samuel my dear, he said, but you have many guides as does everyone, and to call out a name could be confusing you see, for you may think you're talking to me Samuel, when indeed you may be talking to Gloria." "We don't mind, but for your sake guide is all you need."

I liked the name Samuel better than guide, and I thought if each guide would just introduce themselves whenever they appeared then there wouldn't be any confusion. "Well Samuel, I know you now.'"

"You know Samuel, I said, I was reading this book Talking to Heaven while I was waiting for Jack." "I just wasn't expecting to wind up here." "Oh! My dear, he answered, you're not in heaven." He could see the puzzled look on my face as I glanced at him in amazement. Then where the hell, I'm I? I thought. Again with that mental telepathy thing he answered my question. "You're not there either." "There are many, many dimensions, and using your movie terms, you are just in a preview, intermission, so to speak." "Heaven is reserved for those who have left the earthly realm permanently." "Well to me it looks like one of those movies where you're sitting on a cloud and you can look down on earth to see what's going on there." That beautiful warm smile of his was enchanting; I loved it when he smiled like that.

"We can do that, he said, do you want to see?" "Well yes of course" I answered. "Then, he said, as he was holding out an extended hand, follow me." As we stepped out of the water onto sparking sand crystals, I felt myself become completely dry. My gown remembering its beauty, and its luster returned to its original state. Dry in an instant, the permanent press material remembering every little detail, and there I stood once again sparkling like an angel without wings. "I'm not sure this is all good, I said, don't you get bored in a perfect world, nothing to look forward too?" He was laughing out loud now, but at the same time showing me, that there was work that had to be done in these realms as well. The work was something to look forward too, and would leave no time for boredom. It seems that once you're in heavens realm, you choose a task much like a job in order to help your spiritual growth. "Here again you are trying to spread the spiritual spark, and it isn't the ringing of a bell that will get you your wings." "Actually wings are a myth, he said, only the celestial angels in the highest realm have wings." "Does this bother you, he asked, you know you don't need wings if your thoughts can teleport you in an instant."

"I thought heaven was a place to rest, now you're telling me we have to work, hold down a job." He was shaking his head no, but still smiling, I was convinced that he enjoyed my confusion. "You don't have to do anything if you don't want too, but the things you do, to help others, help's your spiritual growth, so most people if not all, choose to help others." "But if they are here do they really need help?" "Yes they do, he answered, but we're talking people like yourself, on earths realm, or on a realm of a different planet much like earth" "So you're saying we are like individual peeking Toms, spying on the living." "Not exactly, he answered, but I'll give you one example!" "There are just too many to mention them all." "Say you're in the hospital where Jack works, and in the nursery there is a new born that isn't long for that realm." "It needs a helping hand to help it back to the realm from which it has just came." "That might be the job you would be asked to do."

"Samuel, I said if there are these people helping others cross-over, why hasn't someone helped Megan, and her boyfriend Tommy? Oh! And I believe my therapist has a mother that still hasn't crossed-over." "What about those people?" "Some, he answered, are untrusting, they have been offered a path of light, but fear has kept them earth bound. Someday they will find their way. Some take many years; hundreds sometimes, while others only a short time goes by before the loving spiritual light guides them home." "Home!" The word had escaped me without thought. "Yes, home he answered, earth was never meant to be home for any of God's people, so when they find their trust, they will return to their creator." "We have heavenly spirits, and earth spirits, like yourself helping to retrieve wondering souls, and that my dear is the only no child left behind act that is bound to work"

No child left behind act, whatever was that supposed to mean, I had never heard of that one before. I was shrugging my shoulders, and shaking my head. The more he talked the more confused I became. "Write it down in your dream genie, he was saying. Somewhere in the future some of the things you hear here will clarify themselves." "Is there more futuristic things I should know about?" I asked. "There are many roads, he answered, we know the end to each one, we even know which one is most likely to be chosen, but there is always the chance, small, but a better decision could be made by a helping hand from a spiritual spark." "What is one of those sparks?" I wanted to know. "Beware of the alien technology, he answered. The one called the Chip." "Oh for sure, that really sounds dangerous." I was laughing as if he had just told the funniest joke of the century, but I was noticing from the expression on his face that whatever this Chip was, it was something to take seriously.

There seemed to be blue sky surrounding us now as we walked the beach completely submerged, more like a fog closing in hugging us with gentle hands. Samuel waved **his** hand, and there was a parting much like and automatic door pushing to both sides. Below us, or above us, or beneath us, wherever, there was the hospital where Jack worked. It was like watching a television screen, Jack was there putting the finishing touches to a plaster cast. A little girl about the age of six, maybe seven, sat quietly not moving a muscle as Jack finished putting the last dab of plaster on her cast. The cast encircled her right hand, and flowed half way up her arm. He lifted her gently to the floor, then offered her a very large red all day sucker. She accepted the sucker with a smile, and a very pleasant low, almost inaudible voice. "Thank you." Jack patted her on the shoulder then turned to talk to her parents, and that was the end. Samuel had waved his hand again, and it was back to the enclosure of the blue mist.

"Jack doesn't talk to me about what he does at the hospital," I was telling Samuel, as we retraced our steps back down the beach. "Whenever I ask him about his day he'll tell me the same old thing" "You know, he'd say, if everybody would stock their medicine cabinet with a big supply of band aids, and aspirins I'd be out of business." "There wouldn't even be a need for that morning phone call." "He just refuses to bring his work home, he'll say, it interferes with the loving atmosphere of home, and there's no place like home." "And speaking of home I was telling Samuel, when Jack gets home, I'll probably still be a sleep in my chair, and the book Talking to Heaven will probably be on the floor somewhere." "Not so, Samuel said, you'll be there in plenty of time to salvage the dinner you have slow cooking in your oven." Oh! I had forgotten about the roast.

When Jack told me he wasn't going to spend the night at the hospital, I popped a small beef roast into the oven, and covered it with a bunch of new Idaho potatoes, fresh carrots, crisp celery, and onions smothered with lots of broth. Slow cooking for five hours that broth was going to make a wonderful, favorable, scrumptious pot of brown gravy. Jack always told me no roast beef dinner should be served without my famous brown gravy. I think he was just prejudice. Being married to me for twenty six years I think he had become accustom to my cooking, for I remembered when we first married, I would hear this doesn't taste like Mom's. I had tasted Mom's cooking, and I was thinking, thank God for that.

Samuel was asking me now if I wanted to see my sleeping body, and I couldn't pass up a chance like that. I was going to see myself in three-D as others saw me, not just an image in a mirror, but as a completely different person. I was shaking my head yes, I defiantly wanted to see that. There was a wave of his hand, a swishing sound, and the parting of what seemed to be sky in front of us, and like before the television screen. We were now focused on home, my home, and there I was sound asleep in my recliner, the book Talking to Heaven open and laying on my midsection. You know, I really looked comfortable. I don't think I had moved an inch, just completely out of it.

Samuel was saying, "You look surprised, is this not what you expected?" "You see he went on, you'll stay as you were when we took you away unless there is a disturbance, in which case you would be pulled back into your body immediately." "So you are actually more aware while gone than you are while there, and sleeping." "Unreal, (that was my reaction, and I was saying it over and over) unreal, unreal." It really looked like me sitting there, but it didn't seem as though it was because here I was, and there was a body that looked like me, but didn't seem at all connected. I was thinking this was what it was going to be at the end of life's cycle, we'll disconnect, and then there will be just one. Maybe we would have duel, or multiple personalities stemming from all the different entities that we were throughout all eternity, but hopefully there will be just one, it would be much too much to deal with if on the top dimension there was many forms of the same person. We could meet ourselves coming and going. Yes I'm talking about reincarnation my view of the wheel of life, excepted or not.

Reincarnation in this day and age is still a taboo subject, and I didn't have time to talk to Samuel about it, not that he would have given me any answers anyway. My experiences in the upper dimensions had to be of my own findings. I was told the answers were there, but the believing was in the finding, and all would be reveled in the end. The time had run out anyway for now the disconnected was reunited, I was awake.

Gazing at the clock on the wall, I realized I hadn't been gone all that long. What seemed like hours had been a few minutes. It's amazing that you can spend what seems like hours, only to find it had been less than a few minutes. Maybe this is why we're told that our lives here on earth seems like only a snap of the fingers to entities on the heavenly realms.

Now I needed to check my roast that was slow cooking in the oven. It was time to settle back into the reality of earth's realm. Jack had insured me that he would be home by ten o'clock. Everything was looking perfect, so I had time to grab my genie book, and start my entries and memories, of what had just transpired. I was writing with enthusiasm not stopping to analyze what I was saying, I needed to fill these pages with the wonderful experiences that I had just experienced. I lost track of the time here, and before I realized it, it was time for Jack to be home. My dear Genie Book had to be put to bed, so I said good night to her, and took up my normal earthly, wifely duties. This was going to be some weird tale to tell Lucy, and maybe even the good Dr. Warren Elliott. There would be no mention to Jack, however a nonbeliever in astral travel.

Jack was so tired from working all the late night shifts this week, that all he wanted to do was have a fast dinner, and fall into bed. Tomorrow would be a busy day getting the ice-skating rink ready for the kids, and grandkids. Halloween wasn't a big concern to him because he knew that was my responsibility, and that was a responsibility that I had well in hand. Lucy, and I had already made plans for the hallowed night, but the spooks and goblins would only serve the two of us. Her children didn't need witches and goblins all they needed was their scary costumes, and candy. So now that the plans had all been laid out, I could hardly wait. Tomorrow night was going to be spectacular.

It was early in the evening of Halloween night when Steve and Lucy came with their tribe of little monsters and ghouls, all the kids screaming trick-or-treat. "So what do you want I asked a trick or a treat?" They just giggled a little as I handed each one a plastic pumpkin filled with all kinds of candy. It was Steve's turn then to take their kids, and disappear into the night. It was time then for Lucy, and me to share our ghost stories, and adventures into the unknown. Halloween was now officially over as all the kids from the neighborhood had just left with Steve. The Yates kids Annie, and Joey didn't show up so with two pumpkins left that meant one for Lucy, one for me. No sense in just having the kids nauseated.

I wanted to begin by telling Lucy about my fantastic journey, my fantastic out-of- body experience, and as usual she listened, fully believing without doubting. I described to her all the beautiful things that I saw." I am so amazed, I said, it's so hard to believe that all the things we've been taught about religion, about God, about the outer dimensions, and everything has all been a fabrication." "I thought the dimension I was in was part of heaven, I told her. However Samuel my spirit guide, tells me no, this is just a preview of what's to come." "Heaven's beauty is far beyond human comprehension." "And Gods dimension is beyond human's mental ability to comprehend." If we are allowed to visit with our deceased loved ones, it's because they have traveled out of their comfort zone, which they are more than happy to do.

Mental telepathy is the way of communicating with the spirit bodies, they all seem to know what you are thinking, but what's amazing is your hearing it all at once, and never does one conversation interfere with the next. What you want to see, and what you need to see is just a thought away. I told her about the beautiful ocean where the Dolphins played at my feet, and where the water was so clear, and beautiful. Samuel told me that it's because humans haven't contaminated the oceans in the upper realms. "Here in your dimension Darby, people are destroying the planet." "The oceans are dying." "The Sea life in your oceans, are dying, and it's only going to get worse." "The oceans, and the heavens above your planet, were never meant to be a dumping ground."

Free will is given when you take human form, even though in your pre-birth charts, you choose what destination you plan to follow in your reincarnated incarnation. It just doesn't say whether or not you will take any responsibility for your planet, this is your free will, and freewill brings difficult changes to the per-birth charts. Pre-birth-charts was definitely something I needed to ask him about, the pre-birth charts again something that Charlotte had talked about in her channeling with her unearthly companions.

He told me for sure that we do in fact choose the life we will lead on this planet however, with free will, it can all be interchangeable as we build in many roadways with exits, detours, and different intersections. You're here to follow your life's path, and complete your life's mission. Some roads will get you to your destination faster than others it just depends on whether you take the high road, the low road, or the road less traveled. It's all up to you, however each, and every road leads to the same final destination. He answered my question here, but he informed me that this was not the plan for my out-of-body traveling, and definitely not the information for my spiritual growth.

I was not aware that I had a plan for out-of-body-travel, or for my spiritual growth, and I wasn't aware of any life mission of predestination. This was something that I was going to find out on my own because he definitely wasn't giving me any clues to whatever these destinations were. I wasn't really in any hurry to find out what these missions were either. I was enjoying the traveling out-of-body. Once you've been to these wonderful far off dimensions you definitely want nothing more than to visit them over and over.

I'm not sure what I liked best about my leaving my sleeping body, and traveling to destinations unknown. I know I love the beautiful skates, and the fact that I can skate like a pro. I like the heavenly music, the beautiful flowers, and the absolutely gorgeous colors. So maybe I don't know why that I have these wonderful Spirit Guides and Guardian Angels, but I am ecstatically happy that they are there. My mission impossible will probably be revealed at a later date, but hopefully not too soon, not if it takes away my special gifts.

The hour was getting late here, and I could tell that Lucy was getting sleepy, she enjoyed our talks, and didn't want to give up the ghost, but I knew she needed to get home, so I told her we had better quit. I needed my sleep too, because tomorrow when the kids and the grandkids arrived I would need a lot of energy. Getting old and being grandparents takes a lot of energy. Jack had been working all day just getting the firewood for his outdoor fireplace, and making sure that the ice was smooth, and ready for the day of family skating. The skating activities with the kids were always the highlights of his day. Tired, and exhausted he comes in says good night, and goes to bed. Now three o'clock in the morning, Lucy is saying her goodbyes. The fire in the fireplace had gone out, so all that was left to do was flip off the lights, and try to sneak into bed without waking my sleeping Jack.

The night was short, but restful, and I enjoyed the peaceful undisturbed rest without the drama of any spiritual connection to the unknown. For a few short hours life seemed normal, and snuggling close to Jack without a single dream of any kind, sleep enveloped my entire existence. Sometimes sleep; pure good normal sleep is a reward in the making. Oh! But the night was way too short, and now I was regretting my decision to spend half of that good night reminiscing about all of the past experiences, and adventures, and keeping Lucy up past her bedtime. The room was starting to fill up with the morning sun, so remembering the old T.V. commercial where the lady was flipping flour in her face, and saying it's time to make the donuts. I knew it was now time to make coffee. I don't make the donuts, I just open the box.

Its morning now and Lucy was late, but Jack was early, so everything worked out perfectly. Jack was fed and out doing whatever the last minute preparations were that he thought needed done, and he wanted everything to be perfect for a spectacular day with the kids, and their skating party.

Lucy and I drink coffee and ate our donuts while we prepared the big container of hot chocolate, and made ready the hot dogs, the marshmallows, the chips, and dips, and the condiments, now we were going to be completely ready for the day of skating as well. Now little after one o'clock in the afternoon the family is starting to show up. Lucy had never planned to stay, and as soon as the family started to arrive she left.

The excitement is running rampant now as the house fills up with the over excited grandkids, they all have their skates, and their warm winter clothes, but first they need to make sure grandpa is ready for them so they can take over his ice-skating rink. It seems they all have to run, and yell, and scream, in order to get reacquainted with their cousins that they haven't seen- in a month or so. Laughing, and giggling, yelling and screaming, there is more excitement in this poor old house than there has been in a long time.

The fire in Jack's outdoor fireplace was amazing all the kids gathered around to toast their marshmallows, their hotdogs, and to drink the hot chocolate. For me I just wanted the blessing of the warm blazing fire to make the outside a more comfortable environment. Watching everybody skating and having so much fun put me in a hypnotic state. I was watching, but daydreaming. Seeing myself in spirit skating, and having fun too! In spirit these things were all possible, but that was spirit, free and without the bulk of the human body, in spirit I was able to stay upright. Now here with the children my skates seemed to have a mind of their own, so wobbling around the rink, trying to protect my backside, and holding on to the pole railing twice around was my limit.

The wooden bench close to the fire is where I would spend the rest of my day. My hypnotic state had me searching far away into the spiritual realms. Even though I was fully awake, when I closed my eyes, I was seeing beautiful streams of water, and waterfalls, oceans bright and clear splashing gently to the shore, and I was imagining myself back in the upper dimension playing with the Dolphins. I just needed to stay focused on our wonderful children, and my beautiful grandchildren, but when spirit calls I am lost to the beckoning's. Here awake but mesmerized I was seeing the skaters, and the heavenly visions simultaneously.

Imagining myself in my beautiful red skating dress, holding the hand of my Guardian Angel, or Spirit Guide whichever the case might be, losing myself so completely to the vision: all I wanted for the day was to stay a normal human in a normal human world. The visions was bringing me closer, and closer to the upper dimensions where my two worlds collide, colliding like in my double lives, or my two lives in one reality. My reality of a double life, or two lives, in one scenario, that where playing out like a movie. I'm lost, I had no choice. I had enjoyed my day with the children, and grandchildren regardless to my flipped upside down double life, and I do believe that they had enjoyed their day, however they were now leaving completely exhausted and worn-out.

CHAPTER SEVEN

It seem the older you get the faster the days seem to disappear, there is never enough time to stuff all of your daily activities into one twenty four hour period. This day was definitely one of those fast, and furious pleasurable days, and now with the day ending, closing its doors behind me, I too was feeling exhaustion. Bedtime was going to be my unwinding. I was definitely looking forward to uninterrupted sleep.

Jack was still enjoying the ice rink. Skating, playing his music, and doing his little dance moves as he glided graciously across what was now an empty rink. I was not going to wait up for him, my bed was calling me.

Warm pajamas, warm bed, and my fluffy pillow, sleep was going to be my only remaining activity. Yet I don't believe I was fully asleep when I heard my name being called. I heard it loud and clear, "Darby." Startled, I open my eyes looked around, but there was no one there, so I settled back on my pillow, and again closed my eyes. "Darby." I heard it again, this time, I saw someone sitting in the huge red stuffed recliner by the side of my bed. To most this would have been a frightening experience, but to me I had become accustom to visitations from the un-embodied. I knew immediately he had to be a Spirit Guide or Guardian Angel, because of the beautiful unearthly light that emanated from his entire being.

He wanted to talk, I wanted to sleep. It wasn't a win-win situation for me. The conversation started with mental telepathy. I started with an open mouth, but was told right away that that wasn't necessary. Most of the conversation was like a silent prayer, but when you're talking to spirit, it's always pleasant, and uplifting, the feeling of never-ending love and joy. I wanted to know why this was happening to me, and he told me because it was something I needed, something that I would need in the future.

It wasn't a question that I was asking, but immediately I started thinking about the Christmas Movie where there were three ghosts, past, present, and future. Immediately his reply was, "Yes, our plan is to keep plaguing you until you have reached your goal." "Then, I asked him, when I reach that goal, are you planning on leaving me?" "That's up to you," he answered. "Our plan is to be here for the duration. "You're freewill will determine the outcome."

Freewill here we go again, I was just living day by day, freewill seemed to be only that of my Spirit Guides and Guardian Angels. These were just thoughts, but he knew exactly what I was thinking. "Everybody has freewill Darby." That was the message I was receiving back in my subconscious mind. "Well why then, do the Spirit Guides or Guardian Angels only show themselves at their will?" "Be aware before you were incarnated you chose to have Spirit Guides and Guardian Angels, we only appear when we feel we're needed." So what was the big urgency tonight, I just needed to sleep?

"The stress of the day as you were visualizing God, and wanting to fly away on your skates, but realizing how impractical that would be leaving your body in a comatose state in front of your family put you in a stressful situation." "Now we would like to take your subconscious mind on a journey." "You wanted to know about the different dimensions, the top dimension, where-God-is, and I'm here to tell you that God is-in every living thing." "He is the living source." "When you think about something that has no beginning, and no end, where would you put the top?" "God is the top, he is everywhere, and everything"

"Now we ask you to close your eyes, breathe slowly, and visualize too your inner self, or the source within." "Visualize the true spark, the true you, feel the energy, and the essence, knowing there is more to the personality than the cloak of physical personality covering the outer body." "Inner-body journeying can be just as rewarding as out-of-body journeying." "To feel the peace, and the love of one's self, and the God source, and the spark which is true spirit, you need to connect with your inner self." "Closing out all the inner voices and the static of the brain releases you from the superficial knowledge of the one-dimensional reality." "You soon realize that there are many realities, and many dimensions connected to your one personality." "So meditate and enjoy the inner-body traveling, there is much to learn from your own Inner Soul." "Remember the journey taken; had to be started one step at a time." "You are way ahead of this journey." "Now a slower pace is called for, a slower pace will bring you a fuller realization of the spirit within." "We bid you a pleasant good night with pleasant journeying to the soul."

With those last few words spoken he was gone. He kept referring to himself as we however I was seeing only one. He had to be referring to all of my Spirit Guides and Guardian Angels collectively. Maybe it was his multi-personalities, and the fact that he is more than one. I was suddenly remembering how my mother used to tell me that life was stranger than fiction. My life was visibly stranger than fiction, so I thought I would just sleep on this, and enjoy the sounds of silence.

The silent part didn't last long however for now I was hearing the sounds of skates being dropped in the hall closet. Jack had given up on his ice-skating rink. He was cold and tired, and ready for sleep. My side of the bed of course was much warmer, and more inviting, so a tug-of-war over warm covers started and lasted for about fifteen minutes. Then there was a total blackout of nothingness, sleep had taken over completely.

The following days with much practice on my quest to practice, and learn meditation, I conquered the task, but found it quite hard. Concentration and staying with the program was not as simple as I would have liked it to be. Meditation didn't seem to be an easy thing for me to accomplish either. For when I closed my eyes all I would see were streams of water, ocean waves, and waterfalls, always water, beautiful streams of water. Usually beautiful white clouds would cover my mind's eye as well, and then I would fall asleep. The voices in my head were saying follow those streams, follow those clouds. I guess in a way meditation had always been a part of my spiritual connection with the universe however, I hadn't carried those visions to the end.

Getting to know the inner-body-source, or the God spark, which I was told was actually the real entity, the real me, the real personality, in which my body was attached, was harder to accept then the out of body experiences that I had come to love so well. The voices spinning around in my head conveying the fact I was not even the person I thought I was. Now as I was watching the images slowly unfolding in my mines eye, and tuning into the vibrations, the sound waves, or vibrations that seemingly had to be telling me, I had learned to soar, to fly, and move freely in the outer dimensions before I had learned to crawl, to walk, or to run. So now what I was being told was I had taken a short intermission from all the soaring out-of-body, a short intermission of baby steps, to the inner-body, and now a spiritual awakening had to be reintroduced to my psyche.

Multiple personalities of life, and past lives seem to be popping up everywhere, and I am seeing past lives, and the possibilities for future lives all at once. This wasn't something that was of a real big interest to me, for once you have learn to fly, to soar, and too experience the freedom of the unencumbered body, the crawling, the stumbling, and the learning to walk seems unimportant. My

Spirit Guides and Guardian Angels were not going to let me get away with this. I was hearing that there was a time, and place for everything, and this was the time, and this was place.

There are many questions forming as I listen to the vibrations, or the knowing of the voices which were actually my higher self, and little by little answers were pouring down like rain drops from the overhead clouds. These knowing voices were like my nighttime visitor, but they were only in my head, they were questions asked by me, and answered by the higher source of my inner body. (Question one.) "When meditating does everybody experiences the same sensations, and the same vibrations?" With that I heard a little laughter, and a simple "No." (Question two) "Why is it that some people experience different messages from meditation?" The answer here was simply, "Because not all people are on the same life path, and their needs are completely different." (Question three) "With the same spark, and the same source wouldn't it be possible that all are just looking for the meaning of life?" "The meaning of life is the true meaning for meditation, however learning one's true self, one's true spark, and the source within are a much more willing, and rewarding journey." (Question four) "Does everybody hear the voices like I'm hearing now when meditating?" Again there was a little chuckle: "Hardly ever does anybody hear the voices of spirit through meditation." "Mostly there are sensations of knowing, of seeing, and of feeling." "Love and joy, and peace bring them closer to the knowing, the source, and the Godhead." "Answers, all kinds of answers can be found while in a meditative state." "Answers to earthly, and heavenly questions can be found through meditation, and it brings a spiritual reality to their body and soul" (Question five) "Why have I been blessed with the audio portion of meditation?" "Meditation requires the stillness of the mind, closing out the rambling, and the clutter that forms complete silence, and serene inner-body piece." "Darby you are not there yet." Since you have learned to fly before you have learned to walk it will be like putting training wheels on your bike now that you have learned to ride." "We have the patients you need, so you need to have the patients with meditation." "True meditation requires complete silence, when you reach this point the voices you are hearing will completely disappear."

What a bummer I didn't want the voices to go away. If I had to learn to meditate, the voices brought from spirit to the inner-body seemed to be a much easier way to go. (Question six) "I'm living on a mountain top in the middle of nowhere, so how is it that my spirit body could have a true and special mission to accomplish?" "Be advised Darby you are exactly where you are supposed to be." "Having a life's plan to follow doesn't mean you have to save the entire world." "There are many earthly angels to follow in the footsteps were the last angel's footsteps ends." (Question seven) "So how is it that I will know what my life's plan is?" "The soul is always aware, you need not worry, the path is starting to unfold, and there is never failure with spirit."

Sometimes I wondered if these voices were from my own subconscious mind, or higher-self, or from the untapped, or dormant part of my brain, or were they really divine interventions. They come in so quiet like whispering in the brain. Maybe I'm just imagining the true validity of the answered questions. With all the pondering, the doubting, and unbelieving it leaves the quest of spiritual enlightenment void, empty, and unfulfilling. I just had to accept the voices as true spirit. It was almost like automatic writing not knowing the outcome until you had read it back.

My eyes were closed now and sleep was overtaking me, I was drifting away into what could have been uninterrupted slumber, however the Guarding Angel, or Spirit Guide whatever he was, was back. With hand extended out to greet me, and me excepting his hand we were off. This time it looked like a long frozen lake ahead of us, all the surrounding scenery covered with snow and looking a lot like a painted Christmas Card. We were skating now, and as usual my feet were supported with the glow of sparkling shiny ice skates. I was dressed in a red skating skirt trimmed in white fur, a red hat trimmed in white fur, but without the tassel that usually supported the white snowball. I looked amazing. Nothing was being said while we skated the long length of the lake until it seemed to just stop. Now we were in a paradise of shining crystal, what a beautiful place, it was breathe taking, and I definitely had to express my amazement!

The things that amazed me about all the out-of-body travels were the sudden changes that occurred. For now I'm dressed in a beautiful white dress with no idea how, or why all of this had taken place. With the Angel beside me now we walked down a crystal walkway where we found a beautiful white crystal bench. This was to be our perch for the duration of this visit. Conversation was strange in these places as I was used to opening my mouth to speak, but my unearthly companion knew all my thoughts, so he answered each and every question as they popped into my head. I had so many questions, and they were all trying to pour out at once. First things first, how were the wardrobes changes taking place, and I heard in my head, you manifested the changes with your own thoughts. That seemed puzzling to me, because I hadn't realized I had that ability, even though I had been told that before.

"Do earth bound spirits have the ability to manifest a change of clothes in this manner?" By asking this I was only thinking of Megan who dressed differently each, and every time I saw her. "They all do, but most don't realize it since most died tragically so they continue to wear their death clothes"

"Now you're thinking Megan in her summer dress aren't you?" "Well that's like your visit with the Dolphins." "She was thinking of a warm summer day, so the rain wasn't affecting her." "She could see your reality, but her reality was her own, and since she doesn't believe she is dead, she continues to live an earthly life in spirit."

"Why hasn't the Angels, or family members come for her?" With that question asked, I was now hearing his voice in my head.

"They have tried, but her belief system concerning the afterlife is shutoff, not allowing her to pass into the light." "That's why you have been appointed for the task, and the Angels know you will find away." I really wasn't all that positive however because I had tried before, and failed. "How about Tommy, I asked, he hasn't left the property since he died in the fire." "With Tommy, he said, it's like the movie, Ground Hogs Day, he is looking for his parents, and each day is the same for him." "The only thing he remembers is the day before, so each, and every day he continues his search." "The house he is seeing today is the house where he died." "He doesn't see the new structure that stands there today." "As he continues his search it might appear that he is walking through walls as the new house is designed much differently."

"Megan is starting to believe and it is scaring her, however she will not leave, and go into the light without Tommy." "Your biggest challenge will be to get Tommy to believe." This was all starting to sound a little like a T.V. rerun. Hadn't I heard all this before? I heard a little chuckle, but no response, so I had to ask what happened to Tommy's parents. Here again it was like De je vu, I learned that they went immediately into the light. I had learned before that Megan's parents had gone into the light, but they managed somehow to return with the idea of getting Megan to follow in their footsteps. Maybe they were just shadow people to me, or bright spirits cloaked in shadow, or ghosts to Jack and Lucy, but ghosts with an agenda all the same.

Still on my mind was the ghost I'd seen in the psychiatrist's office, and as usual my Guide was way ahead of me, and he was explaining that she too was a Spirit Body straight from the Heavenly Realm. I knew she had to be a Heavenly Visitor because of her brilliant heavenly glow. "Warren Elliot's mother he said, and she too has faith in you, she knows that not only does he represent an understanding for you, but that you represent an understanding for him." "She said it will be a healing for both of you." That didn't make much sense to me. I was a doctor's wife, but totally without any healing powers, a little psychic, but not a magician. I was thinking about the appointment with Warren Elliot that was to take place the following week, and thought maybe she would show up again. "No my guide said, she has made her point, the rest is up to you."

"The real reason for your travels tonight Darby, is to reacquaint you with your friends the Dolphins." Well I had met them once on my travels to the upper dimensions, but did that really make them my friends? "Darby, the Dolphins have missed you, you need to remember your past childhood visits with the Dolphins." "You need to remember the wonderful times you had playing with the Dolphins." "They were such a comfort to you and to your little brother when you were young children." I didn't understand this remark. I didn't remember a childhood with the Dolphins, or my brother and I with the Dolphins.

"When you were very young and missing the companionship of your little brother, you used to visit the land of the un-embodied, and traveled to the upper dimensions." "Here you met the Dolphins along with your little brother." "Your family had chosen not to mention your brother after his death as a way to cope with the healing process." "They thought if they didn't mention him, it would help to mend their broken hearts, however too you, there was a need." "You needed more than anything too hear his voice, too see his face, too run and play as you did on earth while both of your earthly bodies slept." "It took some time for you to realize you could leave your world for his and still be able to run and play as usual." "The two of you used to sit by the ocean, where you would run and play in the warm ocean waves, laughing and playing, until you had captured the attention of the loving Dolphins." "It didn't take long for them to become your very best friends" "While hours and hours were spent playing, and swimming with the Dolphins, they never seemed to tire, and were very happy and pleased to have your company."

Oh, so many questions going on in my head, and though he knew what I was thinking, he wasn't giving me the answers I needed. This seemed like a repeat of past travels for never were the questions I had fully answered. "Questions, questions," I said. "What happened, why did this all stop?" "Do you remember the song, Puff the Magic Dragon?" Well of course I did, I loved that song. "It's like that for your brother and you." "As the boy and his Dragon in the song grew older the boy came no more, so with a tearful eye the Dragon slowly vanished away." "Then as the two of you, your brother and you grew older, you came and he was gone." "That's when you suddenly started to disappear, and your brother became your Dragon." "The memories of your un-earthly travels also disappeared, that's why now you are only remembering these visits as dreams" "As you disappeared, you became the Dragon for the Dolphins." "The Dolphins knew that one day you would return, so when you did they were very happy to see you." "Wow! That was so sad. I'm so sorry I didn't remember them."

"What reason did I have for forgetting and not returning?" I asked. It seems to me like Tommy searching for his parents, I'd still be searching for my little brother, my Dragon." He simply stated that all Earth parents convince their young that it wasn't possible to travel out-of-body, and once they were convinced then it wasn't possible, and that's what happened to you. "Most travelers still travel, but they only conceive the travels as dreams, and never recapture the full beautiful experience." "This conversation of the impossible still goes on for kids that see, and hear ghosts, and have invisible friends, they are told it's not possible until they finally believe it's not possible, and they stop believing and grow up to pass on the same message." "What happened to me then, why did I return from dreaming, too out-of-body traveling?" His answer surprised me, "Because, he said, the desire you had was deep seated in your heart, and soul, and the fact is, you are still hunting for your Dragon."

I still had many un-answered questions left to ask, but I could feel the pull of my earth body, and that meant time was running short. The traveling back to the body like before was much more sudden than going forward. It was like a snap of the fingers, and wall–la, home again, home again, gig- a- gig-gig. The next thing I knew I was back in my nice warm bed and Jack was shaking me awake. That had to be the tugging I felt for any interruption to the earthly body was an immediate return trip home. "Hey, Jack why did you wake me up?" "You were having a nightmare, he said, and you were chasing Dragons" I had to laugh a little as I told him. "That's right and I plan to catch that Dragon too, someday."

That had to have been some extra- ordinary, out-of-body experience for my earthly body to experience the sensations felt while I slept, while I traveled out-of-body, while I experienced the love of my lost childhood. That was just something that seemed to be taboo, something that just never, ever happens. The conversations I had had with Spiritual Beings before, had informed me my earthly body would not realize the absence of spirit, and would remain undisturbed until I returned. The trip to the Crystal City was earth shaking, as well as heavenly shaking, for both body and soul, had felt the sorrow, the pain, and the deep desire to rekindle the lost love of my departed little brother Adrian. To rekindle the lost friendship of the Dolphins, who were still in search of their Dragons.

As usual, it had seemed like I had been gone for hours, but actually it had only been a few short minutes. The difference in time between the Universe, and time back on Earth was almost like a year to a day, and now I was remembering what had been said about the aging process on the other side. Spirit grows to adulthood, but never grows old, and those who die old, grow younger. This alone sounds like paradise to me, being twenty nine again would be wonderful, but fulfilling life's challenge's no matter your age has to be the first priority. You never know what Angel duty has been assigned to you. So if you want to earn your wings, be the Angel you were meant to be. This is kind of funny really, because thoughts are your wings on the other side.

It wasn't an easy task falling back to sleep, but the morning sun would soon be pouring through my bedroom window, and Earth life would be calling me back to play the role of the earthling. I couldn't complain, I loved playing both parts of my double life. It just seemed like both worlds were like a stage, and we had to learn the script, and play out our part to bring both worlds together for the completion!

Morning did come, the sun did come up, and life went on as usual, as soon as Jack was off to work my day with Lucy began. After chowing down a box of powdered sugar donuts, and devouring a pot or two of coffee, a lot of conversation took place about astral travel. Then there was finding a way to send Megan and Tommy into the light, which meant we had to take our plans back to the drawing board. Lucy definitely wanted to help the Earth Bound Spirits find their way into the light, as did I, but how? With the following holidays fast approaching there wasn't much time left to work on the extracurricular activities of Megan and Tommy, so all was pushed to the back burner. Spirit wasn't about to let us forget about them thou, so as soon as the Thanksgiving and Christmas Holidays were over, we would have to put our brains in gear, and work on Tommy, who I was told was the problem.

It was time to call Charlotte--that was plan number one. I had always marveled at the differences that each human spirit body possessed. She could talk to the dead and get answers, and she could see their spirit bodies in her mind's eye, yet to have one actually manifest in human form hadn't been one of her earthly talents. One of her most presses talents as she had told us would have been sending un-embodied spirits into the light. Lucy and I were in desperate need of this talent, and her service, so with blackboard up, chalk in hand, the numbered suggestions started rolling out, white over black, numbering one to twenty four.

No need to mention two to twenty four however, for none of them seemed to carry much merit. Plans were just that—Call Charlotte! After calling, and calling we finally got a conformation. Charlotte is just one busy girl. Maybe I didn't want people to know my secret after all. I know I wouldn't be too fawned of my phone ringing off the hook all the time. Now as usual it would be two weeks before she would be able to free up her schedule, and make the trip.

Anyway it was time for Mrs. Darby Mathews to push all spirits and goblins out to the keepers of the universe, plant her feet on Gods good earth, and prepare for one more visit with the good Doctor Warren Elliott. I was getting use to these visits, and now even looking forward to the free time spent just being myself. Well maybe that was it, just being myself, but being in the company of Warren Elliott gave me a peaceful normal feeling, even though he was trying to decide if normal was the right diagnosis.

There was plenty of time before Charlotte's next visit, so relaxing, and enjoying just being the wife of Jack Mathews for a while felt as normal as it gets. Cooking, cleaning, and just catching up on being an Earth Bound Entity. This of course was not nearly as much fun as using your wishful thought power to fly away to the land of the enchanted, but a necessity of my written contract to be a human in human form. This may sound unusual to those that have always been totally Earth bound, but checking the Akashic Records, I have learned that we all have a contract to some degree! That freewill thing takes us off course sometimes, but eventually we all come full circle, and wind up where we were intended to be. There we go round and round, my theory of everything in the universe, including the universe as being a circle.

The circles of life don't seem fair sometimes, and all of us wish that we had made different choices, choices that would have made life more bearable, but we all live, pay taxes, and die. Some of us live with the living, and some of us live with the departed. It's necessary to say departed instead of the dead, because even though the body dies, you yourself will never die. Life is definitely eternal. One more beautiful lesson learned from the Akashic Records!

I have always thought that Warren Elliott was a special life force, choosing a life of helping, and a life, of making a difference. A difference in the lives of those he comes into contact with, but one that is fully under a lot of misconceptions, misguided, and one that could definitely use my shared experiences of out-of-body astral travel. My Spirit Guides have told me that my experiences could help him to understand the circles of his life. His mother of course wanting him to realize that life never dies.

It was only a day away now, so Warren Elliott was all I could think of. I'd sleep tonight, and maybe stay grounded, so as to be ready for his weird questions, mostly forging into my childhood. This would be alright with me, but my childhood was now a thing of the long lost past. So much had happened since I'd seen him last. I wanted to talk to him like Darby does with Lucy Spencer, set him down, and tell him all the wonderful, beautiful things I'd seen while floating out of my body, and traveling to the Way-Stations of Heaven.

One more valuable trip, I had to take, one more trip, before Spirit Guides were going to leave me alone. It seems my last trip had been interrupted before I was giving, and received, the information that seemed most important to all those un-earthly beings. Through default, I had been summed back. It seems it was as much of a surprise to my guides, as it was to me, that my earthly body had felt the sensations that had sent an automatic signal, a signal that brought about a fast departure. Therefore staying grounded wasn't in the play book. Once again I skated off into the Heavenly Way-Stations.

My Spirit Guides have told me that those way stations as I call them are like Suburbs of a much larger city. Each and every one I've visited is in some way my own manifestations. I have never failed to ask how I could manifest these things, when I had no idea of what, or how I did so. The answers sent shivers all through my body! As life is Eternal, I was told, each and every living life force has spent many life times in the Heavenly Realm, so subconsciously the soul body is remembering and manifesting some of the most desired places that you may have visited. Well I guess I'll just leave it to my soul body then, because it seems to be doing a fantastic job. All the way stations, as he was saying, are a total of one, like it says in the Bible. Heaven has many mansions, and all the mansions are a total of one.

While people of Earth are a total of one they fail to recognize their potential, and they continue to fight over religion and politics. They will find no peace until death do they part this world, depart, and enter into the Realms of Heaven where they will learn the full truth of their short comings, and find the truth in the one, and only God.

I think of all the messages I'd received from spirit, I loved this one by far the most, but I still had one more question. "How do people who kill in the name of God find peace in Heaven?" With a smiling face he answered. "Simply, was the answer, they are led through many life time reviews, and shown that they have led many lifetimes of love and compassion." "They are then given the choice to create their own Heavenly Mansion, for in Heaven all is love, and all is forgiven if you are willing to forgive yourself." "The thing to remember is you are your own judge, so judge wisely."

For more questions pertaining to God, I also asked. "Why is it that people here on Earth's Realm have different opinions of their one and only God?" The answer was not in any way what I was expecting the answer to be, but coming from spirit, my spirit guide, I would value it forever more. "Misconception not in one Religion, but in all Religions," was the answer. "There isn't one true Religion anywhere on planet earth, but do not worry, as in Heaven there is no Religion at all." "The people here on Earth's Realm use Religion as a controlling mechanism which seems to work as long as they don't try to blend one with the other." "Live a good life and believe in God, believe in Jesus, and call your God by the name that is right for you." "There is only one God, and all Gods by any other name is the total of one."

There were many more conversations running through my head as I re-entered my sleeping body just in time for the alarm clock to remind me that as an earthling, I must carry on as a spirited body, Earth Bound Entity. Darn and everything was just getting good too!

Warren Elliot, that was the next Earth Bound project, and no I hadn't forgotten about that. The visit to Warren Elliot's office would be one more excitement in the drab life of an Earth Bound Entity. I was getting used to, and enjoying these visits more and more and I didn't even mind the fact that the conversations were all about the past. Anyway for him it was all about the past, but to me it was a heavenly conversation, and I was primed, and full of new information ripe and ready to pour it on him.

The drive to town was always a pleasant trip too, the country side was like natures only hideout. Beautiful trees lined the roadway, and occasionally you would see the wildlife that the foliage had hidden away, that's what it was like today as I entered the valley floor. Just a few miles now, and I would see the welcoming sign, welcoming me into the city. Welcome to Gnome Valley, population Thirty four thousand nine hundred and seventy nine! Sure it seemed like a small amount of people for a town that spread out over the whole valley, but it was a growing community leaving room for a much larger population growth. The warm sun shining through my windshield was making me drowsy, and making me feel like I should just stop and take a nap, but onward I went at top speed, meaning as fast as the law allows. Jack would be furious if I came home with a speeding ticket.

I was still a little early for my appointment, so I stopped off at the little coffee shop on the corner, bought coffee, and a donut then walked down the sidewalk to the office building, and proceeded on to Warren's office. Still I had twenty to twenty-five minutes to wait. Waiting in the waiting room I found a book, a book believe it or not on finding the true spirit within. Finding this book didn't look like a normal thing to find in the office of a psychiatrist, especially a psychiatrist like Warren Elliot, the non-believer. It seemed as though the Universe or my Guardian Angels were trying to help me find just the right way to approach my life-after-death message, a message of confirming my belief system. I thought this was want was expected of me, for my mission was not for letting his mother down, but for bringing Warren up. My Spirit Guides, or the Universe, wherever the driving force seemed to be, was a force that was driving me, making it necessary for me to keep returning month after month. Returning just to be convinced my life was nothing more than a fantasy.

I didn't need to read this book: My life as an Astral Traveler was the best teacher anybody could ever ask for. It appears that Warren may have had this book in his waiting room from his first day in office, maybe that's where I had read it before. Whatever the case, I was guessing it would stay until the pages were no longer readable. I flipped through the pages, and then tossed the book down; this waiting was by far too much. Each minute as the time clicked by seemed more like an hour. But patience pays off, the time had come, and my name was now being called.

Warren was standing alongside his desk with an outstretched hand welcoming me, and thanking me for waiting, and calling me his favorite patient. "Please don't call me a patient Warren, I said. Call me a client, if you call me a patient it makes me feel like you are already working on comment papers or something" "Not for you Darby he answered, not for you." So after the motioning to sit and the awkward greeting was over. It was once again question and answer time. Warren as usual came with note pad and pen.

This always reminded me of my dream genie, knowing you can't do anything without the memory log.

"Well today is Monday, Darby he said, I guess you spent your day yesterday at your favorite Church, I'm I right?" I didn't respond to that remark as he knew from our past sessions that I wasn't one to run off and spend my time in Church, astral travel, but not Church. That was just his way of opening the conversation, getting me wound up so I'd start revealing more of my private life as he called it, the probing into the deep psychotic mind of the mental patient. While it did set off the time bomb I'd been holding back on, surprising even to me. I started revealing my last visit to the Astral World. This was a subject that normally I tried to avoid for a while, because it seemed to confirm more need for therapy.

"So there has been a little astral traveling going on since we last met?" And I just continued with my speech as though he hadn't even asked. The last visit to the Astral World was so amazing that I was sure he would be impressed with my description of those unearthly realms. I was telling him about the Crystal Way Stations. The Crystal Way Stations of course was what my Spirit Guide had called them. Yes I told him, my Spirit Guide have told me that all the realms that I had visited were just Way Stations, and that the only actual Heavenly Realm ever entered into was the library where the Akashic Records were kept. I told Warren about calling the realms suburbs to the larger city, and asked my Spirit Guides why there wasn't more unearthly spirits there, it always seemed so quiet without humans. There were animals, insects, and lots of plant life, but usually never any spirits of the dead.

"What answer did you get to that?" Warren asked. "I was told that even though those realms were spectacular, and very beautiful, they could never in anyway compare with what is yet to come." "This I told him was a surprise to me because I couldn't even imagine anything anymore spectacular than this beautiful Crystal Realm, the Crystal Way Station." "Then I was told that the departed spirits preferred the higher realms as they all had many things that they wanted to do, and the higher realms provided them with the opportunity of their desires."

What I learned on that visit was how everything is connected, but the spirit world was preparing me for a much bigger, and needed spiritual awakening. That seemed the most important of all things to reveal, what more could there be? The experiences are what I wanted to talk about, so telling Warren about my experiences in the Astral World had to be revealed. I was telling him what My Spirit Guides had told me, that everything is connected, all the people are like one, all the Gods are one because there is no other than one, the Universes are like one, everything is one. "Wow" That was the response I got from Warren, and of course he wanted me to explain the oneness of it all. If like, I said, I was in the Astral Realm, how is it I didn't already know about all the awakenings that spirit had to offer?" That I couldn't explain, but I could do a little repeat of what my Spirit Guide had to say on the oneness.

My Spirit Guide revealed to me that the oneness is like a ball of twine, you can unroll it, but it's still all one piece, each and every person is a part of the twine. "Then why, asked Warren, is there so many different personalities, you know what I mean, why is there both good and bad people, wouldn't they all be the same?" "I was told that since the people, all the people have freewill they go about their lives living, and doing whatever they think is best for them." "Evil exists because of this freewill." "Good people might think something bad is going to happen to them so they continue to think about it, and thinking about it makes it happen." "There has to be someone willing to take on the evil roll that you have imagined." "It's all in your thoughts, what you think becomes your reality, you design your life with your thoughts."

I heard once before you had to be careful with your thoughts, but it was my belief that our thoughts were private and couldn't hurt anybody. However in Astral Travel you learn that thoughts are a living thing, and you manifest your reality with consistently thinking about what is going to happen. On this realm the negative out ways the positive because you give it more energy, the constant worrying about something helps to manifest it into your reality. "Well then Darby, all this tells me is that your constant thinking about astral travel really means you are manifesting a fantasy" "I'm sorry I can't believe in astral travel, but it certainly seems real to you, but real to you doesn't make it so." "There is so much that needs to be done here, and it's something I haven't dealt with before." "I'm sure if we keep working on your belief system we can find a way to bring you down to earth." "Down on solid ground, to where, you can live a normal life!" Well that's the same answer he had before, I'm not normal. I live in a fantasy world.

With his research into my dysfunctional life style, he was still asking questions, and still wanting to know about my belief on the oneness of all the Gods. That too, I said was like a ball of twine and all the names that Religions call their God is still only one. The ball of twine fits on top of the other ball of twine, and then it's like a tree with the roots that goes down into all the oneness of the other, making everything a total of one. We have the Earth, the Gods, and the Universes, everything imaginable all rolling in and out making a total of one. As the Spirit Guide was explaining it to me in this manner, I was imagining the top ball of twine as the top dimension, however I was told that when something is eternal there is no beginning, and there is no end, so therefore there is no top or bottom, just the oneness of it all. I was still imagining the idea that Heaven is the highest of all realms so therefore had to be the top dimension. The top dimension he said is everything rolling into one, the oneness is your top, all oneness of dimensions, is still only one dimension.

Now Warren wanted to know why all the people here on Earths Realm had so many different interpretations of the one God, where some see him as all good, and others see him sometimes as not so good. Misinterpretation I was told, all the Church's misinterpret the scriptures, and fill in the blanks with whatever seems to please their way to believe. That's why you see different ideas in each religion, some are good, and some quite the opposite! However they all feel they are following God's law, so they fight to protect their beliefs. All truth shall be revealed on their departure from human to spirit, I'm told, for only truth resides in Heaven. "Well if they are wrong, and practice the laws which they think are of God, but are not of God, do they still go to Heaven?" "I don't know I can't judge, but I'm pretty sure that all will return to the source of God" "We are just here to learn, and if we do it wrong, we will just have to return, and try again." Warren was shaking his head, and repeating over and over, "amazing, amazing, amazing!"

Warren's disbelieving mind was convincing him this had to be fictional, and could not hold any truth at all. "Darby this astral traveling thing you say you do isn't possible." "This has to be all dreams, or wishful thinking; people just don't fly off the Earth's Surface, and talk to Spirit Guides or Guardian Angels, it just isn't a thing that a normal person, or any sane psychiatrist would do." "So when awake here on this planet what do you do with your day?" I really didn't want to answer that, because the more I talked the more insane it seemed. What was I going to say, Oh! Lucy and I send the dead into the light? That was our next project, and something we weren't quite sure was going to work. I was really thankful that our time was running out, and I could take my un-normal insane dysfunctional body and leave.

I really wanted to talk to my Spirit Guide right then, I wanted to ask him what was really going on here. Why wasn't I getting anywhere with this guy? Nothing seemed to soak in with him, and I was quite positive that whatever it was I was supposed to be doing here was far beyond my expertise. I glanced at the clock on the wall, still fifteen minutes of probing time, I could be deemed totally insane by then. Talking about universal way stations and un-embodied spiritual travel was sounding a little outlandish even to me. Getting this impossible speech over and over made me think maybe I should just keep all my secrets bottled up. I knew Astral Travel wasn't impossible, I lived it, it's my life. If I stalled here a little bit I'd be free to go maybe without the help of a strait jacket. This seemed to be the way I felt each and every time I visited this guy. He always made me feel so crazy!

I was always excited about my arrival, for that's what I was always looking forward too, but escaping once the hour started was ever more of a blessing. I had seen his handsome face, and felt the deep spiritual connection. The spiritual connection that made my life fulfilling, and complete. I would see him again in two weeks and again I would be overjoyed with the anticipation. I could be deemed crazy, but that didn't seem to matter. To be sane or to be crazy, it usually takes a psychiatrist to drive you completely nuts. If you're sane when you start out, plan on a complete reversal by the time your sessions are over. I really liked this psychiatrist, and that gave me the courage to open up, and talk quite openly with him, despite the fact that his analogy was always the same, meaning, it's all impossible! Now he was still asking questions, so I had to sit quietly and watch the exit sign, and hope, I didn't fail all his tests.

"Darby when you talk like life never dies, how I'm I suppose to respond to that?" "Well I guess you just go with it, and except the fact that life is eternal, and someday you will see your mother again." "She sure wants that to happen, not right away you know, but when it's your turn to leave this realm for the next." "Now he said you are talking like you have been in contact with my mother!" "I think I'm going to prescribe a mild medication, and I really feel that you should take it." He was scribbling on his prescription pad all the while he was talking, but I knew I wasn't going to take it. People just don't screw up a good life with drugs. How many people can claim to live two lives at a time, one on Earth, and one in the Astral? My Spirit Guides say it can be done, but for most it would take a lot of concentration. For me it was handed down like an inheritance no work at all, just a good night flight of dreams. Now who in their right mind would take drugs for that?

I took the piece of paper from his hand, and said my good-byes, stopped at the receptions desk made a new appointment and left. However the wadded piece of paper in my hand found its way into the nearest garbage can. Knowing that without medication I'm free, I'm free as a bird, and I can still take flight. I'm most thankful for the Astral World, for my dreams, for my traveling, and my eager, and willfulness that bring all the pleasure, and pure delight. There is no way I'd give that up, whether I'm having an hallucination, or truly experiencing the most magnificent out-of-body sensational journey of a life time. These were my times, the times away from earthly obligations, to holidays no other human will ever dare to take. Such a pity that Warren's psychiatrist training omits the supernatural, leaving him void of all realities beyond the five senses. Maybe if I talked to Jack, maybe he would loosen the strings on my so called strait jacket, and let me fly free. No more crazy talk at the crazy office. Although, I knew I didn't want that to happen.

There was the sign leaving Gnome Valley, I was half way home now, and my brain was still trying to convince me to never go back, never ever go back. I must have been driving subconsciously thinking about what a waste of time the last hour had been. It always seemed that way, but somehow when the time arrived, I'd always find my way back, it was back and forth, like a puppet on a string, following the puppet master. I couldn't give that up, I was addicted!

Home now I was having trouble with the key in the door, and the phone was ringing. Alright I'm coming, I said don't hang-up. The key was upside down how stupid of me, but I made it to the phone on time. Charlotte's voice was saying, "I was just about to hang-up. I tried calling a couple of times before, but there was no answer." I was just getting home I told her, but without any mention of my bumble fingers placing my key upside down in the lock. Our conversation lasted about two hours, small talk for the two of us, with nothing important being said other than in three days she would be headed my way to help with my ghost problems, sending Tommy and Megan into the light.

Not once had I ever seen Tommy, but I knew I was going to miss-Megan, she had been a friend before, and even after I realized she wasn't a living entity, a living entity, living in my realm, but that she was still very much alive. "You are always alive my spirit guides had told me, spirit never dies." That was a comforting thought; still it would be a sad departure for me, but hopefully a happy reunion for Tommy and Megan, and happy reunion for their loving families.

Three day waiting period now was expected for the project of sending Megan and Tommy into the light. Three days waiting for our good friend Charlotte. I hated the waiting. Three days always seemed like a month when all you have to do is imagine the outcome, the magnitude, of a project we had no idea would work, could we really pull this off. Is this really going to work? The next thing to do was preparing my scared little neighbor Lucy, for what she was going to call an adventure of a life time. Not to brave that one, but still she wanted to be a part of the departure.

This was another one of those nights when Jack was on call at the hospital, so as usual he was going to spend the night in town. So after a quick shower, and a change into a clean pair of pajamas, I called Lucy. "I'll be right over she said. I have a box of powdered sugar donuts, so if you have a beverage to go with them, that would be wonderful." "I'll see you in a few." She meant coffee of course, but Steve was probably listening, so beverage was the word. Coffee and donuts always a good treat no matter what time of day or night it might be. The sun was still shining on the mountain top so the evening was still young, we still had a long visit, and she was home before dark, not that the dark meant anything between the two houses. Just a quick skip, and a jump, and she would be safe at home.

Everything seemed to be falling in place, so nothing left to do but close my eyes, and see what might manifest from there. It was always a guessing game. It might be a peaceful night of sleep, or travel time. After an hour or two of tossing and turning I then knew, it was travel time. My body was resting peacefully, while the real part of me, my spirit body, was off to its next adventure.

Something was different this time, there was a spirit guide helping me depart the Earthly Realm, helping me enter into the realm of spirit, but there were no ice skates on my feet. A stone pathway leading through a beautiful forest land stretched out before us. What a beautiful site this was. If on Earth's Realm the forest looked like this nobody would want to cut, or destroy a single branch. We walked without talking for a while, then we set down on a bench that looked like another of the forest trees that had grown, and had shaped itself into this beautiful bench. No matter how many times I've enter into the realm of spirit, I have always been amazed at the beauty. Birds were singing in the tree tops not just a tweet, tweet, tweet, but what sounded like a harmonizing quartette. We were communicating, the spirit guide and me, but it was more like mental telepathy.

I was being told how pleased the spirit world was that I had taken on the role of Earth Angel, taking and agreeing to help send Tommy and Megan into the light. Then of course I wanted to know why it was up to an earthling, and not the spirit world, and here again, I was told the story of Tommy and Megan's belief that they were still alive.

Tommy and Megan believing they are still alive will not listen to the spirit entity's that have been there, and have tried, so it will take an Earth Angel, someone on earth alive, and in earth body to convince them. Megan, I am told believes, but she will not leave Tommy for the light.

Tommy searches the house all the time looking for his mother and father, which are not there anymore, going through doors that are not there anymore, as he sees the house as it was before the fire. The new house was designed completely different, however in Tommy's mind it is still the same. The new tenants believe the house is haunted, because they can sometimes hear the slamming of doors, that are not there anymore, and they are also hearing other weird noises that can't be explained.

It was a total repeat, of spiritual messages which didn't seem at all necessary, and I could have still been at home sleeping peacefully. The thought was more of a gratitude statement, however as they were conveying the faith they had in me and my earthly team of helpers, this trip like always was completely necessary. It was a reminder that as an earth bound humanly entity, there was still heavenly work to be done.

"The unseen spirits will be there Darby, giving you all the help that is available, but remember we have faith in you." "We feel you are the best Earth Angel for this job, and one of the reasons we have been guiding you, giving you insights into the important visions of the spirit realm" "Heaven's Realm is more spectacular than anything you have seen so far, so will be a gift of eternity for two deserving Earth Bound Spirit Entities." "A little push from an Earth Bound Angel, is all that's needed here." "We have faith in you."

This was the last message I received from this Spirit Guide, as the alarm on my clock radio was buzzing. I sat up, put my feet on the floor, and stared in amazement at what I was seeing now. Standing there and in full body was my departed little brother. I hadn't seen him since he departed the land of the Dolphins. I couldn't believe this, I was awake, fully awake, this had never happened before. Whenever I saw Adrian before it was always in the Spirit World. This was earth shaking, and I was in a cold sweat, cold but sweating. He was smiling at me, and then he said, "I'm not your little brother anymore, I am somebody else now, but I still love you" That was all he had to say, turning to his side he was gone, and standing there in his place was- Warren Elliot. "I know you." "You're Warren Elliot," I said. Without another word, any word at all, and with only a smile Warren Elliot disappeared also. This was so unbelievable, reincarnation-Adrian- verses- Warren. How could that be? Warren the unbeliever in reincarnated, yet I saw it, it had to real!

Unbelievable this was reincarnation we were talking about now. How could I refuse to believe when I saw this with my own eyes? Warren Elliot didn't seem to believe in live after death much less reincarnation! So many questions now running through my mind should I tell him, or should I just keep this to myself? I can't explain how, or who it really was that was standing there giving me this message. Was it Adrian's Spirit Body, or Warrens Spirit Body, or a Spirit Guide relaying the message that I so needed? Whatever now the decision was should I, or should I not, tell Warren what just happened?

Whatever decision I would make would have to wait as the spirit world wanted first and foremost for me to work my magic on Tommy and Megan. Charlotte was on her way. Lucy was hiding somewhere in the shadows whispering let's do this thing. Lucy is so cute, you just have to love her, she wants to be brave, but only if she can hide behind me and Charlotte.

It was only a day away now. Charlotte's arrival would mean putting all our plans on the drawing board once again, and deciding the best program to follow since all three of us had our own ideas to the final departure route.

CHAPTER EIGHT

Lucy had spent all morning with me now as we waited for Charlotte. Of course we had devoured a full box of powdered sugar donuts and finished off a couple pots of coffee. With full tummies it seemed more like nap time, but the long wait was over, as Charlotte had finally arrived. Sitting around the kitchen table we talked about Tommy and Megan, and what their spirit life seemed to be. It wasn't until I mentioned Tommy's obsession with rattling closed doors, searching behind doors, and continually looking for his parents that the light bulb in Charlottes head seemed to light up. "That's it she said, if we can contact him, get his attention long enough we can convince him that the door he is looking for is in the light." "Once he enters the light it will be over, because his parents will be there." Lucy and I both had to agree that that might work. How about Megan, Lucy asked. "What will happen to her?" "She will follow Tommy, I'm sure." "Darby has told me, Megan wants to go, but she doesn't want to leave Tommy behind." "Get Tommy and we've got them both." That was our plan then, the next few hours was spent talking about our lives, and catching up on the living. Not to say that the deceased were not living, more like they were invisible to those that had yet to become deceased. Life is eternal, that was the subject we had talked about over and over, and now we had to make sure that Tommy and Megan lives their life eternal in the upper dimension.

The day was slipping away so it was now or never. Charlotte's car was already out in the driveway so our choice of transportation was easily settled. Lucy was already starting to look a little pale and I knew she was going to be my shadow for whatever time our project was about to take. We were about to find out, for we were already there, the home of the Warrick's, slowly making our way to the front door.

Oh! There was that spooky door knocker, the Skull–and–Crossbones, the one that vibrated making the spooky booming sound. I had to look around to find Lucy. I should have known where she would be, she was hiding behind me. Even a shadow couldn't have been any closer. It was only a minute, but seemed like five before Susan made her way to the door, of course she met with Charlotte first, and after their introductions, Charlotte introducing herself as Charlotte Hutchinson, Susan then told Charlotte her name Susan Yates. Susan's two small children, the baby Joey was in her arms, and her little girl Annie was hanging on to her skirt tail. That reminded me of Lucy, that little four year old girl was just as brave.

Susan seemed very happy that we were there, and she knew immediately why, so she gave us her permission to do whatever we needed to do. She told us she would talk to her husband Fred and have him turn off the television. She definitely didn't want anything to interfere with our progress.

The search was on, and I really didn't feel optimist, for the first hour didn't turn up any visions of ghostly activity, but then I thought I caught a glimpse of Megan. If only I could talk to her for just a minute, I was sure this visit would prove profitable. I started talking to her, and I knew she was listening. "Megan I said we are here to help Tommy find his parents, but we need you to help us." Megan wasn't saying anything, but I knew she heard me, so I continued to talk to her. "Please listen I said, Tommy's parents are in that big bright light can you see it?" "We need him to go there please help us." There was silence for a short time then suddenly Megan was there, I could see her plainly. "Megan I said, you and Tommy should go on into the next dimension, it is so beautiful there." "I've seen it." It is where you need to go. You will find your parents, and all your loved ones there." "Help us please Megan." "What do I say to him?" It was Megan talking finally." "Tell him behind the light there is a door." "Tell him it is the door he has been looking for, and tell him you know his parents are there, he will listen to you." Megan made a little motion with her hand, and I saw Tommy. He was so young looking, and I felt like I was looking at Casper the friendly ghost for he had beautiful blonde hair and big blue eyes. "He said he will check it out." That was Megan again passing on the message from Tommy.

"Can you see the light? "I asked. "No" she said. "Then ask! I said. Say Spirit Guide show me the light." "Oh now I see it, that worked." "Then go I said, take Tommy and go." As strange as this was, I could see both Tommy and Megan hand in hand disappearing into the light. They were gone, and my Angel duty on Earth was over. "So now what, Spirit Guide I asked. Where do I go from here?" Asking that question didn't work for me however, I didn't get an answer.

After saying our good-byes to the Yates family, and driving back down the mountain, I told the girls I really did appreciate having their help. I think I would have given up if it hadn't been for Charlotte. Lucy of course was the silent partner, but Charlotte was like a Chatty Kathy Doll, always giving me advice, and telling me what to say, and how to say, what was needed to be said. We did it, and we were quite pleased with ourselves. The spirit guides should stop now with their Angel on Earth speech, and just let us live normal human lives. Was that too much to hope for?

The daytime light was gone now, and a big full moon lit the forest, what a beautiful sight to behold. With the day over, Charlotte agreed to spend the night. Jack was late as usual so we had a BBQ party on the patio. The Spencer's Lucy and Steve both came over, and the rest of the night we talked about whose steak was the biggest, and whose was the juiciest. The chilled bottle of wine however had to just keep chilling until Steve and Lucy had gone home. Well I know what you are thinking, but you can't serve a Mormon wine.

Jack was happy when he found he had a full bottle of chilled wine to go with his perfectly cooked Filet Mignon, and the neighbors had already gone home. It was a good meal, a hot bath, and then passing out in a warm bed for the rest of the night. A perfect life for a hardworking man, I would say. This was the way our married live had been going for a while, but then I had more than enough to keep me busy, so there were no complaints.

I showed Charlotte to the guest room where she crashed on the bed and fell sound asleep without even taking off her shoes. Ghost hunting must really be an exhausting adventure for my girl Charlotte. Maybe I'm keeping her up way beyond her bedtime, because that happens every time she stays the night.

Noticing the bottle of wine on the table, and seeing that there was still a glass, or maybe a glass and a half left in the bottle, I decided to drink until the end. This wasn't a usual thing for me, but the night seemed young, so out to the patio with my wine, and reclining in a lounge chair watching the big full moon, and starlit night, I finished it off. The next thing I knew it was morning, and Jack was making the morning coffee.

Charlotte wanted to go shopping of all things. Do you think this head of mine was going to cooperate? There was a buzzing sound going on in there. Now it was bacon, pancakes and coffee, and off to the big city. I had to admit the big breakfast did help, and the shopping trip was pleasant. I thought I was doing just fine, but Charlotte kept hushing me as I talked to some of the other shoppers. "Come on Darby, she would say." It wasn't until we were on our way back up the mountain side, that she told me that no one else could see the customers I was talking too.

It must have been embarrassing for her to be with someone acting so strange. Although as strange as it was, Charlotte managed to buy a complete new outfit. She was complaining about wearing the same outfit home, that she had slept in all night, but now she looked amazing, and she was ready to drop me off at home. Charlotte reminding me anytime I wanted to talk to invisible friends, she would be very glad to come help me out. "Hopefully we are through with the strange stuff, I told her, but strange actions require strange company, so I'll keep you in mind." She laughed, waved, and then she was gone.

Lucy was waiting for me, and perched in the same lounge chair where I had spent the night. Coffee was the main goal for this visit she had to have her coffee. I, on the other hand had to pretend to be hospitable, while I envisioned myself sitting in the hot tub, dreaming about floating away, forgetting about all of yesterday's problems. Peace, and quiet, was my dream, with no neighbors, no friends, and no Spirit Guides, just me, and a very hot and bubbly hot tub. How wonderful it would be, dreaming while soaking in the hot bubbly waters. I needed the leisure alone time, just me, and my hot tub. It would have to wait as life seemed like a marry-go-round—what happened yesterday repeating itself today. Lucy wanted to visit! The day did finally dissipate, however leaving me alone with my favorite desire, the hot bubbly water, but not for long.

"Oh, come on," is what I remembered saying, for what was happening now was unreal. I was being pull out of my body. A Spirit Guide and I were skating toward a way station in the next dimension, holding on tight to the hand of this persistent Spirit Guide who wasn't about to take no for an answer. It might have seemed like I was grumbling, not wanting to leave the comfort of my hot tub, but he was laughing at me as he pointed back down at my sleeping body fully submerged in the hot bubbly water. "You are resting, he said, so now come with me."

I thought these trips would probably be over now, I had learned that my little brother had been reincarnated, and I was successful in sending Tommy and Megan into the light. What more could there be? I hadn't said that out loud, but as usual he knew what I was thinking, and I was told that the next lessons were scheduled to begin. My next question to him was. "Did I really agree to all this before I was born, or are you just making this up as we go along." "A little of both, he laughed, you and your little brother sat down together before birth, and decided this life style." "You have much more to do, and this will not end until this life time ends." "Adrian isn't a part of this life anymore, I said, so if it was for the two of us, why is it still happening?" "He is still alive." "You are still alive, it is still happening."

I hadn't been noticing the beautiful surrounding until now. I guess I was too busy complaining about being disturbed from my leisure time. It was just time to stop and smell the roses, they were everywhere. "Roses are a sign of love, he said, so we are showing you are love and gratitude." "We had all the needed faith in you." "We also know that you are not as willing to give up on Astral Travel as you think you are right now." "We will be here whenever the need arrives." I was cool with that. I loved these out-of-body trips no matter how inconvenient they might seem at the time. The roses here could be handled without the little thorny pricks that accompanied roses on dimension one, or is our dimension-dimension zero. Eternity is a hard thing to figure out. Given a few more out-of-body trips maybe the truth will be revealed. I was told once all would be revealed in the end.

I was convinced that Adrian wasn't going to be a part of my life here anymore either, whether we call him Adrian, or we call him Warren. I was asking does Adrian have any memory of his out-of-body experience coming to me in this life time. "Before Adrian was reincarnated into the new life as Warren, he signed a new contract giving him a one-time trip to meet with you" "He will not be doing that again." "Contract, what do you mean, I asked. Does everybody sign a contract before they are born?" "Yes was the answer." "Yes, that wasn't an answer that just means we have no freewill." "You have freewill Darby, the contract means you have certain things to do." "The Spirit Guides are always there trying to help." "Why do we need your help? Why can't we just do it?" "Well do you remember the contract you signed with Adrian before your birth?" "No, I said, I really don't."

"Let me explain then." "That would be good please enlighten me." I think I was getting a little agitated at the thought of having no freewill. "Both you and Adrian sat down, and made the agreement, it was the only way to be together. "Adrian and you both knew that his life would be short." "It wasn't pleasant for either of you, but you wanted to be together, so the contract was signed." "He continued on even after returning to spirit bringing you into the astral realm to share with you the beauty of the spiritual realm." "This continued until the day he chose to be reincarnated." "Before he signed his new contract, he asked for more visitations with you, and he was allowed one."

"Does everyone sign a contract before they are born?" "Yes" again was the answer. "Everyone signs a contract to do certain things, but not everybody has the same goals in mind, so some are small, and others are much greater." "The problem, he said, when returning from spirit to an earth entity there is no memory of any contract." "Upon your return to earth from spirit you are given Guardian Angels and Spirit Guides, this too is something most people don't have any knowledge of, so their task will be much harder." "You are only to ask if you are to receive." "With the freewill sometimes the contract is not honored, so it becomes incomplete." "An incomplete contract brings you back through reincarnation."

"Adrian what about Adrian, I said, wasn't his contract complete?" "Very much so, but through freewill you have the right, and are given the chose to be reincarnated. He wanted to come back for you. The thought was neither of you knew how hard his departure would be for you." "You prayed for his return, and it was heard."

Wow! That was a big chunk of news to be throwing at me. It was my fault that Adrian had to return from his beautiful heavenly home, back to earth, for what, a onetime visit. "You have had many visits with him haven't you Darby." "Yes I have but he doesn't know." "It was for you Darby, he said, Adrian knew that once you knew, the pain you couldn't give upon for so many years would go away, that was his gift to you, and the completion of his new contract." "If his contract is complete will he be called back to spirit?" "No he will live a long full life this time, but reincarnation may not be a thing he will ever want to do again."

"These roses are so great, and they smell so good, can I take one back with me?" He was smiling at me as he told me. "These roses are alive here to take one back with you, it would die, it would have to be the desire of the rose if that was to happen." "No then I don't want that to happen." "I should leave them here where they can live." "I don't want to be responsible for another spirit leaving its heavenly home."

I felt a little thump on my forehead, and with a startled reaction I was back in the warm bubbling hot tub. There was a rose floating in the water, but I'm not sure it was from heaven, it didn't have any steam, or thorns anything at all. My guess is it was an earth grown flower, and I had just sent this earth grown flower to heaven.

Heaven was great, the hot tub was heavenly, but definitely time to move to a drier land. Slipping my robe on, wrapping a towel around my wet hair, and leaving wet foot prints all the way to the glass sliding door. I was off to save my earth grown rose.

All you need to know about life was just ask and you will receive. You know just one request away! I'm still trying to understand pre-birth contracts, pre-birth arrangements, and freewill. Well what if we want to change our minds once we get here, are we doomed to follow the pre-arranged plans? It seems like if everything is known beforehand why bother playing it out at all.

This had just been a day to grumble, so now here I was sitting in front of my bed room mirror talking to myself. What I needed to do was dry this wet hair, and go to bed. After a good night's sleep, and my out-of-body astral traveling's had been processed, my depression would probably go away, making me feel more down to earth where the normal life would most likely kick in.

Sometimes when you talk to yourself you get answers from spirit you weren't expecting, and now I was getting a response to my grumbling. More times than not when you see people talking to themselves, and they seem to be getting responses, you start thinking to many drugs. I was actually hearing the same voice of the same Spirit Guide that had just taken me on a walk through a rose garden. So to quote this is what I was hearing. "Darby your life is not pre-destined, you are not puppets on a string, controlling your destiny comes from your own thoughts." "Spirit doesn't control thoughts so if you don't like the life you are leading change is up to you."

I loved the life I was leading. I was just in a depressed mood which happens sometimes. You can't be perfectly happy all the time, but his interfering into my thoughts right then put a sudden stop to my grumbling. You can't have rose gardens all the time, but when you do the experience is spectacular.

There are many lessons to be learned from spirit if you just allow the quiet, and the stillness to manifest, and except the invisible, yet audible voice of your Spirit Guides. This was hard for me at first, but over the years of out-of-body-travel, spending time with spirit, seeing a world unseen to most, I have come to grips with Earth versus Spirit. The separation or separate entities, Earthly Bodies, versus, the Realistic Spirit Bodies. WE are spirit entities having an illusion-al experience in a human body. Everything we do as human, in the human body is for the good of spirit. Our pre-birth-plan is what leads us to the truth of who we are, and why we are here. I have no idea why spirit wanted me to add that at this time, but there it is.

It's been my life up till now, and now spirit wants to talk. So for a brief intermission from getting from start to finish I will allow that to happen. So please enjoy what spirit has to say, and remember as a spirit body, and a per-birth-planner it has always been up to you.

"Greeting Darby, We have talked to you on the Astral Plane, and we continue to talk to you here on Earths Plane, we hope that you will understand that all the pre-birth- planning has been for your spiritual growth. Your brother Adrian chose in this life, and his previous life, as a way to help you with evolving back to soul" "This may sound strange, but evolving is an essential part of all wanting to reconnect with source." "Your soul remembers all the personalities you have lived throughout all your incarnations." "Evolving back to soul is the way, the only way of finding your top dimension."

"Each incarnation of a soul on earth longs for this evolving whether they are aware of soul, or not." "Now if you choose to tell Adrian what you have learned, that would be solely up to you." "We do not advise you to do so, you might regret that decision." "It was never meant for him to be part of your life in this incarnation." "Adrian was training you to astral-travel in his past life, his only way of communicating with anyone throughout his short incarnation, now he does not remember this." "His mission in this incarnation was for you also, he has met the demands of his per-birth-contract, and he is now free to live, and enjoy all the rest of this life, all the while giving more as an Earth Born Angel."

"One final message for you here, your training as an astral-traveler will not be diminished." "Throughout this incarnation you will be tested time, and time again, and as you learn from your travels your spirit body will be in search of evolving back to soul" "Evolving the only definition of searching for the top dimension."

Well that seemed like a lot to digest, we are the spark, and the light of the source looking to reconnect. Looking around at the people on the planet today that may take some time. Not judging here, just saying since most are not aware of their purpose of life, it will take longer for them to evolve.

CHAPTER NINE

At this point I have spent many appointments with Warren always trying desperately not to share my visions of his strange out-of-body visit. How do I know if it was even him, maybe it was his spirit guide! If I told him, and he was in total disbelief then I would have no other choice than to terminate all future visits, just continuing to remember he wasn't meant to be part of my life, again in this life time.

I still have my astral travel, maybe in some distant future; we might find a future-life where we might share our lives again, even if it's only in the unseen dimensions. I miss the Dolphins, and I miss Adrian, but just knowing that he lives, and that he has a good life, proves to be a blessing. Maybe I can let go now.

Back at my little breakfast nook I was pouring out more than coffee, I was sharing more than donuts, I was pouring my heart out to Lucy. I had to tell somebody, and here she was, this little tiny person taking it all in. I have to admit she didn't have the knowledgeable mind to deal with the spirit realm, or the out-of-body travel, but she always showed a great deal of interest, and always willing to give free advice. So more coffee, more donuts, and more advice, but it was not to end there. It went from my long ago deceased little brother to my now living three children, whom Lucy felt should take my full attention. The living rather than the departed, the living that needed their mother, and she knew, the mother that, needed the attention of the three living children.

I loved my three children, but they all had lives of their own now, and only seemed to have time for Dad and Mom whenever Jack polished off the ice skating rink. I loved seeing them skate, and I loved seeing all the grandchildren. This always reminded me of the old saying that my mother used to say. "A daughter is a daughter all her life, but a son is only a son until he takes a wife." I was telling Lucy maybe I should try my astral travel to visit them. They wouldn't know I was there, and I could hear their excuses as to why the visits to mom and dad were so few and far between.

I had never tried to visit a place on the home dimension so that was something I was tempted to try. My spirit guide told me my astral travel would not be diminished. "Well you might be surprised what you can do if you try." Lucy was still giving me sound, and strong advice, and we talked way into the night. It was close to midnight before Jack finally arrived, showing signs of being over worked, tired and hungry. Jacks arrival always put an abrupt end to the girl talk, so Lucy slipped silently out the front door.

Being the good wife, I fixed Jack a sandwich out of left over BBQ chicken, and gave him a big scoop of potato salad, and watched as he tried to eat, and keep his eyes open at the same time. After a quick shower he was off to bed, and I was left with the mess, and my conscious fight to reveal, or not reveal the vision of reincarnation to Warren. I was losing the battle. There was another appointment coming up in three days and my mind was made up. I couldn't keep it to myself any longer. As far as astral traveling to my children's house I knew that was out, somehow that seemed like spying, and that wasn't my style. If anybody is into astral traveling the upper dimensions is the ultimate. My home away from home, I'm sticking to the upper dimensions. I'd love nothing more than to see Adrian, and the Dolphins in the astral realm once again, but I know now I had to give that up.

Waiting wasn't something I had much patience with either, I wanted the time to be sooner not later, I wanted Warren to know why our lives had been drawn together. It seemed to be another pre-life destination for a pre-birth-planning. So to ignore the spirit guides warning, my decision was finalized. They had told me, it was all up to me, telling him might be something I would regret, but I had to take the chance. Regret, or not too regret, I was about to expose all my weirdness, in what was about to become my last and final appointment, and leave a part of my heart in the office of a true earthbound psychiatrist.

The day had arrived, and now I was standing in front of the office door. Warren Elliot's name seemed to be flashing like a neon sign. This should have been my warning. I should have taken heed. I didn't want my time with Warren to end so abruptly. Though he would never feel the true spiritual connection that I was feeling, I was desperate to keep our friendship, our relationship, our true spiritual connection, which was a part of what was left of our lives here on Earth's Dimension.

Having Adrian, or should I say Warren, in my life again for such a short time, felt like a true spiritual blessing. Adrian's short life as my baby brother had been one of the most pleasurable experiences that any five year old could imagine. Now with three years of therapy with my psychiatrist whom I believe to be the reincarnation of Adrian, our time on Earth again was about to end.

Sitting in the recliner pouring out my heart to this nonbeliever, and watching the expression on his face, knowing our time here in this life time had come to an end, brought a flood of tears rolling down my cheeks. He was so different, different than he was at the age of three, with one life time removed. The true spirit of Adrian was gone, but the true essence, the true spirit, the true living life force, was still Adrian. Adrian or Warren it was a blessing, I will always hold close to my heart. I would always and forever love them both—as one. Where life after life always goes on, maybe we will live a life together again, in a future incarnation.

Warren had slipped a disk of disconnect into his memory bank when he entered into this present day incarnation, there was absolutely no memory of any past lives, no memory at all traveling out of body to inform me that he was now the reincarnation of Adrian. He was making me feel psychotic. I had to be delusional people just don't reincarnate. I was hearing this over and over in my subconscious mind. I'm delusional, we don't reincarnate, we live one life and that's the end. "We are born, we live, we pay taxes, and we die." "If there is an afterlife it's on judgment day."

The Spirit Guides were right. I should have just remained silent. I should have never told him at all! The doubting look returned to his face as I explained all of the truths that had been shown to me. He couldn't wrap his mind around the far-out belief system of reincarnation. His patient, the crazy astral-traveler, surly needed more therapy, and more guidance. I had spent my entire hour trying to convey the truth; he so bluntly refused to accept. The dreaded feeling now, was it was truly over. I wanted to cry, for our one time visit had come to an end, and I knew he would never know, or believe, anything until life's end. The end where all will be revealed!

The voice in my head still telling me I should have taken heed to the warning of my spirit guides and let this conversation stay a part of my spiritual existence. I felt myself struggling to find the outdoor. I didn't stop to make a new appointment this was it. I knew there would be no more. I don't remember getting on the elevator or the walk to my car, I just remember sitting there with my head on the steering wheel wanting to escape the embarrassment, I felt so ashamed.

I was feeling the pain, and the shame, but knowing that spirit is everlasting brought me some comfort, and a new awakening. I had been drawn to the spirit body of Adrian, due to our pre-birth-charts, now it had to end. This could be the reminder that all spirit life is a total of one, and all spirit bodies are eternal, and a total of one. Even the Alien life that was met in the sleep walking dimensions was no doubt evolving the same as earth bound entities. We are all living life sources searching and evolving back to the God Source, which is the source of all. The source of eternity, and the knowing it is our eternal home. Mine Adrian's, and yours!

I wanted Adrian to know me again in this life, it just didn't happen. When we meet again in the upper dimension I'm sure he will respect the fact that I tried, but failed, to make him understand. My time in this dimension is much shorter than his, and I'm sure to watch over him until his time comes to an end. I really hope that he lives a long and happy life, and he can forget that once he had the craziest of all crazy patients as a client.

Sitting in my car now, all the pain, and sorrow of losing Adrian, once again had returned. How long I sat with my head on the steering wheel, I will never know. It was the bright light I was seeing making me realize maybe I had died. That would truly have been a blessing at that time. I felt myself traveling toward that light at an accelerated speed. I wasn't sure what was going on, it was the only conscious thought I'd had since leaving Warrens office. There was a figure, a bright figure, so bright, so beautiful, and so loving. I kept going toward that figure in the light, but he stepped forward, and I was stopped. "It's not your time Darby, you have to go back." But I didn't want to go back. Never in all of my astral travel, had I felt this much peace and loving energy. However it was too late to argue for without any warning, I was back. My head still propped against the steering wheel.

As I drove toward home and going through the residential streets of town, I couldn't help but notice for the first time how many statues of Gnomes there were in peoples yards, and I wondered how many times some of these Gnomes may have by the hands of strangers done a little traveling on their own, only to return with pictures of faraway exotic Earthly Places.

I had heard so many strange, but true stories about people stealing the little Gnomes, taking them on their vacation, where they photographed all their worldly travels. While on the run, the Gnomes could have spent many weeks, or months traveling, leaving their owners wondering just what happed. Then suddenly they were returned. Always with photos, proof in fact, that they had indeed traveled the globe.

People here in Gnome Valley must truly be proud of their little community to display the hundreds of little Gnome Statues that I was observing as I drove so slowly through the residential streets. There haven't been a lot of strangers traveling through our community so it's doubtful not many, or any, of the little Gnomes here have had the opportunity to travel. Gnome Valley is a very small and unobserved place on the map.

Like the Gnomes however if by the hands of strangers that have taken me on exotic unearthly journeys, I could return with pictures maybe my adventures, and stories, could be more readily observed. But for now I have to go with what my spirit guides have told me, all will be revealed in—THE END.

Phyllis Sinclair Author for comments or questions e-mail
(alwaysalive@centurylink.net)

Short story description: A paranormal story about Astral-Travel or
out-of-body travel. Spirit guides and Guardian Angels. Spiritual
Dimensions above and beyond Earth and Reincarnation.

Printed in the United States
By Bookmasters

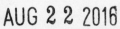